The Two Noble Kinsmen

William Shakespeare and John Fletcher

Table of Contents

The Two Noble Kinsmen

William Shakespeare and John Fletcher

THE TWO NOBLE KINSMEN:

Presented at the Blackfriers
by the Kings Maiesties servants,
with great applause:

Written by the memorable Worthies of their time;

Mr. John Fletcher, Gent., and
Mr. William Shakspeare, Gent.

Printed at London by Tho. Cotes, for John Waterson:
and are to be sold at the signe of the Crowne
in Pauls Church-yard. 1634.

(The Persons represented in the Play.

```
Hymen,
Theseus,
Hippolita, Bride to Theseus
Emelia, Sister to Theseus
[Emelia's Woman],
Nymphs,
Three Queens,
Three valiant Knights,
Palamon, and
Arcite, The two Noble Kinsmen, in love with fair Emelia
[Valerius],
Perithous,
[A Herald],
[A Gentleman],
[A Messenger],
[A Servant],
[Wooer],
[Keeper],
Jaylor,
His Daughter, in love with Palamon
[His brother],
[A Doctor],
[4] Countreymen,
[2 Friends of the Jaylor],
[3 Knights],
[Nel, and other]
Wenches,
A Taborer,
Gerrold, A Schoolmaster.)
```

PROLOGVE.

[Florish.]

The Two Noble Kinsmen

New Playes, and Maydenheads, are neare a kin,
Much follow'd both, for both much mony g'yn,
If they stand sound, and well: And a good Play
(Whose modest Sceanes blush on his marriage day,
And shake to loose his honour) is like hir
That after holy Tye and first nights stir
Yet still is Modestie, and still retaines
More of the maid to sight, than Husbands paines;
We pray our Play may be so; For I am sure
It has a noble Breeder, and a pure,
A learned, and a Poet never went
More famous yet twixt Po and silver Trent:
Chaucer (of all admir'd) the Story gives,
There constant to Eternity it lives.
If we let fall the Noblenesse of this,
And the first sound this child heare, be a hisse,
How will it shake the bones of that good man,
And make him cry from under ground, 'O fan
From me the witles chaffe of such a wrighter
That blastes my Bayes, and my fam'd workes makes lighter
Then Robin Hood!' This is the feare we bring;
For to say Truth, it were an endlesse thing,
And too ambitious, to aspire to him,
Weake as we are, and almost breathlesse swim
In this deepe water. Do but you hold out
Your helping hands, and we shall take about,
And something doe to save us: You shall heare
Sceanes, though below his Art, may yet appeare
Worth two houres travell. To his bones sweet sleepe:
Content to you. If this play doe not keepe
A little dull time from us, we perceave
Our losses fall so thicke, we must needs leave. *[Florish.]*

4

Actus Primus.

[Scaena 1.] (Athens. Before a temple.)

*[Enter Hymen with a Torch burning: a Boy, in a white Robe before
singing, and strewing Flowres: After Hymen, a Nimph, encompast
in
her Tresses, bearing a wheaten Garland. Then Theseus betweene
two other Nimphs with wheaten Chaplets on their heades. Then
Hipolita the Bride, lead by Pirithous, and another holding a
Garland over her head (her Tresses likewise hanging.) After
her Emilia holding up her Traine. (Artesius and Attendants.)]*

The Song, *[Musike.]*

Roses their sharpe spines being gon,
Not royall in their smels alone,
But in their hew.
Maiden Pinckes, of odour faint,
Dazies smel−lesse, yet most quaint
And sweet Time true.

Prim−rose first borne child of Ver,
Merry Spring times Herbinger,
With her bels dimme.

5

Oxlips, in their Cradles growing,
Mary–golds, on death beds blowing,
Larkes–heeles trymme.

All deere natures children sweete,
Ly fore Bride and Bridegroomes feete, *[Strew Flowers.]*
Blessing their sence.
Not an angle of the aire,
Bird melodious, or bird faire,
Is absent hence.

The Crow, the slaundrous Cuckoe, nor
The boding Raven, nor Chough hore
Nor chattring Pie,
May on our Bridehouse pearch or sing,
Or with them any discord bring,
But from it fly.

*[Enter 3. Queenes in Blacke, with vailes staind, with imperiall
Crownes. The 1. Queene fals downe at the foote of Theseus; The
2. fals downe at the foote of Hypolita. The 3. before Emilia.]*

1. QUEEN.

For pitties sake and true gentilities,
Heare, and respect me.

2. QUEEN.

For your Mothers sake,
And as you wish your womb may thrive with faire ones,
Heare and respect me.

3. QUEEN

Now for the love of him whom Iove hath markd

The honour of your Bed, and for the sake
Of cleere virginity, be Advocate
For us, and our distresses. This good deede
Shall raze you out o'th Booke of Trespasses
All you are set downe there.

THESEUS.

Sad Lady, rise.

HIPPOLITA.

Stand up.

EMILIA.

No knees to me.
What woman I may steed that is distrest,
Does bind me to her.

THESEUS.

What's your request? Deliver you for all.

1. QUEEN.

We are 3. Queenes, whose Soveraignes fel before
The wrath of cruell Creon; who endured
The Beakes of Ravens, Tallents of the Kights,
And pecks of Crowes, in the fowle feilds of Thebs.
He will not suffer us to burne their bones,
To urne their ashes, nor to take th' offence
Of mortall loathsomenes from the blest eye
Of holy Phoebus, but infects the windes
With stench of our slaine Lords. O pitty, Duke:
Thou purger of the earth, draw thy feard Sword

That does good turnes to'th world; give us the Bones
Of our dead Kings, that we may Chappell them;
And of thy boundles goodnes take some note
That for our crowned heades we have no roofe,
Save this which is the Lyons, and the Beares,
And vault to every thing.

THESEUS.

Pray you, kneele not:
I was transported with your Speech, and suffer'd
Your knees to wrong themselves; I have heard the fortunes
Of your dead Lords, which gives me such lamenting
As wakes my vengeance, and revenge for'em,
King Capaneus was your Lord: the day
That he should marry you, at such a season,
As now it is with me, I met your Groome,
By Marsis Altar; you were that time faire,
Not Iunos Mantle fairer then your Tresses,
Nor in more bounty spread her. Your wheaten wreathe
Was then nor threashd, nor blasted; Fortune at you
Dimpled her Cheeke with smiles: Hercules our kinesman
(Then weaker than your eies) laide by his Club,
He tumbled downe upon his Nemean hide
And swore his sinews thawd: O greife, and time,
Fearefull consumers, you will all devoure.

1. QUEEN.

O, I hope some God,
Some God hath put his mercy in your manhood
Whereto heel infuse powre, and presse you forth
Our undertaker.

THESEUS.

O no knees, none, Widdow,
Vnto the Helmeted Belona use them,
And pray for me your Souldier.
Troubled I am. *[turnes away.]*

2. QUEEN.

Honoured Hypolita,
Most dreaded Amazonian, that hast slaine
The Sith–tuskd Bore; that with thy Arme as strong
As it is white, wast neere to make the male
To thy Sex captive, but that this thy Lord,
Borne to uphold Creation in that honour
First nature stilde it in, shrunke thee into
The bownd thou wast ore–flowing, at once subduing
Thy force, and thy affection: Soldiresse
That equally canst poize sternenes with pitty,
Whom now I know hast much more power on him
Then ever he had on thee, who ow'st his strength
And his Love too, who is a Servant for
The Tenour of thy Speech: Deere Glasse of Ladies,
Bid him that we, whom flaming war doth scortch,
Vnder the shaddow of his Sword may coole us:
Require him he advance it ore our heades;
Speak't in a womans key: like such a woman
As any of us three; weepe ere you faile;
Lend us a knee;
But touch the ground for us no longer time
Then a Doves motion, when the head's pluckt off:
Tell him if he i'th blood cizd field lay swolne,
Showing the Sun his Teeth, grinning at the Moone,
What you would doe.

HIPPOLITA.

Poore Lady, say no more:

I had as leife trace this good action with you
As that whereto I am going, and never yet
Went I so willing way. My Lord is taken
Hart deepe with your distresse: Let him consider:
Ile speake anon.

3. QUEEN.

O my petition was *[kneele to Emilia.]*
Set downe in yce, which by hot greefe uncandied
Melts into drops, so sorrow, wanting forme,
Is prest with deeper matter.

EMILIA.

Pray stand up,
Your greefe is written in your cheeke.

3. QUEEN.

O woe,
You cannot reade it there, there through my teares—
Like wrinckled peobles in a glassie streame
You may behold 'em. Lady, Lady, alacke,
He that will all the Treasure know o'th earth
Must know the Center too; he that will fish
For my least minnow, let him lead his line
To catch one at my heart. O pardon me:
Extremity, that sharpens sundry wits,
Makes me a Foole.

EMILIA.

Pray you say nothing, pray you:
Who cannot feele nor see the raine, being in't,
Knowes neither wet nor dry: if that you were

The ground–peece of some Painter, I would buy you
T'instruct me gainst a Capitall greefe indeed—
Such heart peirc'd demonstration; but, alas,
Being a naturall Sifter of our Sex
Your sorrow beates so ardently upon me,
That it shall make a counter reflect gainst
My Brothers heart, and warme it to some pitty,
Though it were made of stone: pray, have good comfort.

THESEUS.

Forward to'th Temple, leave not out a Iot
O'th sacred Ceremony.

1. QUEEN.

O, This Celebration
Will long last, and be more costly then
Your Suppliants war: Remember that your Fame
Knowles in the eare o'th world: what you doe quickly
Is not done rashly; your first thought is more
Then others laboured meditance: your premeditating
More then their actions: But, oh Iove! your actions,
Soone as they mooves, as Asprayes doe the fish,
Subdue before they touch: thinke, deere Duke, thinke
What beds our slaine Kings have.

2. QUEEN.

What greifes our beds,
That our deere Lords have none.

3. QUEEN.

None fit for 'th dead:
Those that with Cordes, Knives, drams precipitance,

Weary of this worlds light, have to themselves
Beene deathes most horrid Agents, humaine grace
Affords them dust and shaddow.

1. QUEEN.

But our Lords
Ly blistring fore the visitating Sunne,
And were good Kings, when living.

THESEUS.

It is true, and I will give you comfort,
To give your dead Lords graves: the which to doe,
Must make some worke with Creon.

1. QUEEN.

And that worke presents it selfe to'th doing:
Now twill take forme, the heates are gone to morrow.
Then, booteles toyle must recompence it selfe
With it's owne sweat; Now he's secure,
Not dreames we stand before your puissance
Wrinching our holy begging in our eyes
To make petition cleere.

2. QUEEN.

Now you may take him, drunke with his victory.

3. QUEEN.

And his Army full of Bread, and sloth.

THESEUS.

Artesius, that best knowest
How to draw out fit to this enterprise
The prim'st for this proceeding, and the number
To carry such a businesse, forth and levy
Our worthiest Instruments, whilst we despatch
This grand act of our life, this daring deede
Of Fate in wedlocke.

1. QUEEN.

Dowagers, take hands;
Let us be Widdowes to our woes: delay
Commends us to a famishing hope.

ALL.

Farewell.

2. QUEEN.

We come unseasonably: But when could greefe
Cull forth, as unpanged judgement can, fit'st time
For best solicitation.

THESEUS.

Why, good Ladies,
This is a service, whereto I am going,
Greater then any was; it more imports me
Then all the actions that I have foregone,
Or futurely can cope.

1. QUEEN.

The more proclaiming
Our suit shall be neglected: when her Armes

Able to locke Ioue from a Synod, shall
By warranting Moone–light corslet thee, oh, when
Her twyning Cherries shall their sweetnes fall
Vpon thy tastefull lips, what wilt thou thinke
Of rotten Kings or blubberd Queenes, what care
For what thou feelst not? what thou feelst being able
To make Mars spurne his Drom. O, if thou couch
But one night with her, every howre in't will
Take hostage of thee for a hundred, and
Thou shalt remember nothing more then what
That Banket bids thee too.

HIPPOLITA.

Though much unlike *[Kneeling.]*
You should be so transported, as much sorry
I should be such a Suitour; yet I thinke,
Did I not by th'abstayning of my joy,
Which breeds a deeper longing, cure their surfeit
That craves a present medcine, I should plucke
All Ladies scandall on me. Therefore, Sir,
As I shall here make tryall of my prayres,
Either presuming them to have some force,
Or sentencing for ay their vigour dombe:
Prorogue this busines we are going about, and hang
Your Sheild afore your Heart, about that necke
Which is my ffee, and which I freely lend
To doe these poore Queenes service.

ALL QUEENS.

Oh helpe now,
Our Cause cries for your knee.

EMILIA.

If you grant not *[Kneeling.]*
My Sister her petition in that force,
With that Celerity and nature, which
Shee makes it in, from henceforth ile not dare
To aske you any thing, nor be so hardy
Ever to take a Husband.

THESEUS.

Pray stand up.
I am entreating of my selfe to doe
That which you kneele to have me. Pyrithous,
Leade on the Bride; get you and pray the Gods
For successe, and returne; omit not any thing
In the pretended Celebration. Queenes,
Follow your Soldier. As before, hence you *[to Artesius]*
And at the banckes of Aulis meete us with
The forces you can raise, where we shall finde
The moytie of a number, for a busines
More bigger look't. Since that our Theame is haste,
I stamp this kisse upon thy currant lippe;
Sweete, keepe it as my Token. Set you forward,
For I will see you gone. *[Exeunt towards the Temple.]*
Farewell, my beauteous Sister: Pyrithous,
Keepe the feast full, bate not an howre on't.

PERITHOUS.

Sir,
Ile follow you at heeles; The Feasts solempnity
Shall want till your returne.

THESEUS.

Cosen, I charge you
Boudge not from Athens; We shall be returning

Ere you can end this Feast, of which, I pray you,
Make no abatement; once more, farewell all.

1. QUEEN.

Thus do'st thou still make good the tongue o'th world.

2. QUEEN.

And earnst a Deity equal with Mars.

3. QUEEN.

If not above him, for
Thou being but mortall makest affections bend
To Godlike honours; they themselves, some say,
Grone under such a Mastry.

THESEUS.

As we are men,
Thus should we doe; being sensually subdude,
We loose our humane tytle. Good cheere, Ladies. *[Florish.]*
Now turne we towards your Comforts. *[Exeunt.]*

Scaena 2. (Thebs).

[Enter Palamon, and Arcite.]

ARCITE.

Deere Palamon, deerer in love then Blood
And our prime Cosen, yet unhardned in
The Crimes of nature; Let us leave the Citty
Thebs, and the temptings in't, before we further
Sully our glosse of youth:
And here to keepe in abstinence we shame
As in Incontinence; for not to swim
I'th aide o'th Current were almost to sincke,
At least to frustrate striving, and to follow
The common Streame, twold bring us to an Edy
Where we should turne or drowne; if labour through,
Our gaine but life, and weakenes.

PALAMON.

Your advice
Is cride up with example: what strange ruins
Since first we went to Schoole, may we perceive
Walking in Thebs? Skars, and bare weedes
The gaine o'th Martialist, who did propound
To his bold ends honour, and golden Ingots,
Which though he won, he had not, and now flurted
By peace for whom he fought: who then shall offer
To Marsis so scornd Altar? I doe bleede
When such I meete, and wish great Iuno would
Resume her ancient fit of Ielouzie
To get the Soldier worke, that peace might purge
For her repletion, and retaine anew
Her charitable heart now hard, and harsher
Then strife or war could be.

ARCITE.

Are you not out?

Meete you no ruine but the Soldier in
The Cranckes and turnes of Thebs? you did begin
As if you met decaies of many kindes:
Perceive you none, that doe arowse your pitty
But th'un—considerd Soldier?

PALAMON.

Yes, I pitty
Decaies where ere I finde them, but such most
That, sweating in an honourable Toyle,
Are paide with yce to coole 'em.

ARCITE.

Tis not this
I did begin to speake of: This is vertue
Of no respect in Thebs; I spake of Thebs
How dangerous if we will keepe our Honours,
It is for our resyding, where every evill
Hath a good cullor; where eve'ry seeming good's
A certaine evill, where not to be ev'n Iumpe
As they are, here were to be strangers, and
Such things to be, meere Monsters.

PALAMON.

Tis in our power,
(Vnlesse we feare that Apes can Tutor's) to
Be Masters of our manners: what neede I
Affect anothers gate, which is not catching
Where there is faith, or to be fond upon
Anothers way of speech, when by mine owne
I may be reasonably conceiv'd; sav'd too,
Speaking it truly? why am I bound
By any generous bond to follow him

Followes his Taylor, haply so long untill
The follow'd make pursuit? or let me know,
Why mine owne Barber is unblest, with him
My poore Chinne too, for tis not Cizard iust
To such a Favorites glasse: What Cannon is there
That does command my Rapier from my hip
To dangle't in my hand, or to go tip toe
Before the streete be foule? Either I am
The fore–horse in the Teame, or I am none
That draw i'th sequent trace: these poore sleight sores
Neede not a plantin; That which rips my bosome
Almost to'th heart's—

ARCITE.

Our Vncle Creon.

PALAMON.

He,
A most unbounded Tyrant, whose successes
Makes heaven unfeard, and villany assured
Beyond its power there's nothing, almost puts
Faith in a feavour, and deifies alone
Voluble chance; who onely attributes
The faculties of other Instruments
To his owne Nerves and act; Commands men service,
And what they winne in't, boot and glory; on(e)
That feares not to do harm; good, dares not; Let
The blood of mine that's sibbe to him be suckt
From me with Leeches; Let them breake and fall
Off me with that corruption.

ARCITE.

Cleere spirited Cozen,

19

Lets leave his Court, that we may nothing share
Of his lowd infamy: for our milke
Will relish of the pasture, and we must
Be vile or disobedient, not his kinesmen
In blood, unlesse in quality.

PALAMON.

Nothing truer:
I thinke the Ecchoes of his shames have dea'ft
The eares of heav'nly Iustice: widdows cryes
Descend againe into their throates, and have not

[enter Valerius.]

Due audience of the Gods.—Valerius!

VALERIUS.

The King cals for you; yet be leaden footed,
Till his great rage be off him. Phebus, when
He broke his whipstocke and exclaimd against
The Horses of the Sun, but whisperd too
The lowdenesse of his Fury.

PALAMON.

Small windes shake him:
But whats the matter?

VALERIUS.

Theseus (who where he threates appals,) hath sent
Deadly defyance to him, and pronounces
Ruine to Thebs; who is at hand to seale
The promise of his wrath.

20

ARCITE.

Let him approach;
But that we feare the Gods in him, he brings not
A jot of terrour to us; Yet what man
Thirds his owne worth (the case is each of ours)
When that his actions dregd with minde assurd
Tis bad he goes about?

PALAMON.

Leave that unreasond.
Our services stand now for Thebs, not Creon,
Yet to be neutrall to him were dishonour;
Rebellious to oppose: therefore we must
With him stand to the mercy of our Fate,
Who hath bounded our last minute.

ARCITE.

So we must.
Ist sed this warres a foote? or it shall be,
On faile of some condition?

VALERIUS.

Tis in motion
The intelligence of state came in the instant
With the defier.

PALAMON.

Lets to the king, who, were he
A quarter carrier of that honour which
His Enemy come in, the blood we venture

Should be as for our health, which were not spent,
Rather laide out for purchase: but, alas,
Our hands advanc'd before our hearts, what will
The fall o'th stroke doe damage?

ARCITE.

Let th'event,
That never erring Arbitratour, tell us
When we know all our selves, and let us follow
The becking of our chance. *[Exeunt.]*

Scaena 3. (Before the gates of Athens.)

[Enter Pirithous, Hipolita, Emilia.]

PERITHOUS.

No further.

HIPPOLITA.

Sir, farewell; repeat my wishes
To our great Lord, of whose succes I dare not
Make any timerous question; yet I wish him
Exces and overflow of power, and't might be,
To dure ill–dealing fortune: speede to him,
Store never hurtes good Gouernours.

PERITHOUS.

Though I know
His Ocean needes not my poore drops, yet they
Must yeild their tribute there. My precious Maide,
Those best affections, that the heavens infuse
In their best temperd peices, keepe enthroand
In your deare heart.

EMILIA.

Thanckes, Sir. Remember me
To our all royall Brother, for whose speede
The great Bellona ile sollicite; and
Since in our terrene State petitions are not
Without giftes understood, Ile offer to her
What I shall be advised she likes: our hearts
Are in his Army, in his Tent.

HIPPOLITA.

In's bosome:
We have bin Soldiers, and wee cannot weepe
When our Friends don their helmes, or put to sea,
Or tell of Babes broachd on the Launce, or women
That have sod their Infants in (and after eate them)
The brine, they wept at killing 'em; Then if
You stay to see of us such Spincsters, we
Should hold you here for ever.

PERITHOUS.

Peace be to you,
As I pursue this war, which shall be then
Beyond further requiring. *[Exit Pir.]*

EMILIA.

How his longing
Followes his Friend! since his depart, his sportes
Though craving seriousnes, and skill, past slightly
His careles execution, where nor gaine
Made him regard, or losse consider; but
Playing one busines in his hand, another
Directing in his head, his minde, nurse equall
To these so diffring Twyns—have you observ'd him,
Since our great Lord departed?

HIPPOLITA.

With much labour,
And I did love him fort: they two have Cabind
In many as dangerous, as poore a Corner,
Perill and want contending; they have skift
Torrents whose roring tyranny and power
I'th least of these was dreadfull, and they have
Fought out together, where Deaths−selfe was lodgd,
Yet fate hath brought them off: Their knot of love,
Tide, weau'd, intangled, with so true, so long,
And with a finger of so deepe a cunning,
May be outworne, never undone. I thinke
Theseus cannot be umpire to himselfe,
Cleaving his conscience into twaine and doing
Each side like Iustice, which he loves best.

EMILIA.

Doubtlesse
There is a best, and reason has no manners
To say it is not you: I was acquainted
Once with a time, when I enjoyd a Play−fellow;
You were at wars, when she the grave enrichd,

24

Who made too proud the Bed, tooke leave o th Moone
(Which then lookt pale at parting) when our count
Was each eleven.

HIPPOLITA.

Twas Flaui(n)a.

EMILIA.

Yes.
You talke of Pirithous and Theseus love;
Theirs has more ground, is more maturely seasond,
More buckled with strong Iudgement and their needes
The one of th'other may be said to water *[2. Hearses ready*
with Palamon: and Arcite: the 3. Queenes. Theseus: and his
Lordes ready.]
Their intertangled rootes of love; but I
And shee I sigh and spoke of were things innocent,
Lou'd for we did, and like the Elements
That know not what, nor why, yet doe effect
Rare issues by their operance, our soules
Did so to one another; what she lik'd,
Was then of me approov'd, what not, condemd,
No more arraignment; the flowre that I would plucke
And put betweene my breasts (then but beginning
To swell about the blossome) oh, she would long
Till shee had such another, and commit it
To the like innocent Cradle, where Phenix like
They dide in perfume: on my head no toy
But was her patterne; her affections (pretty,
Though, happely, her careles were) I followed
For my most serious decking; had mine eare
Stolne some new aire, or at adventure humd on
From musicall Coynadge, why it was a note
Whereon her spirits would sojourne (rather dwell on)

25

And sing it in her slumbers. This rehearsall
(Which ev'ry innocent wots well comes in
Like old importments bastard) has this end,
That the true love tweene Mayde, and mayde, may be
More then in sex idividuall.

HIPPOLITA.

Y'are out of breath
And this high speeded pace, is but to say
That you shall never like the Maide Flavina
Love any that's calld Man.

EMILIA.

I am sure I shall not.

HIPPOLITA.

Now, alacke, weake Sister,
I must no more beleeve thee in this point
(Though in't I know thou dost beleeve thy selfe,)
Then I will trust a sickely appetite,
That loathes even as it longs; but, sure, my Sister,
If I were ripe for your perswasion, you
Have saide enough to shake me from the Arme
Of the all noble Theseus, for whose fortunes
I will now in, and kneele with great assurance,
That we, more then his Pirothous, possesse
The high throne in his heart.

EMILIA.

I am not
Against your faith; yet I continew mine. *[Exeunt. Cornets.]*

Scaena 4. (A field before Thebes. Dead bodies lying on the ground.)

*[A Battaile strooke within: Then a Retrait: Florish. Then
Enter Theseus (victor), (Herald and Attendants:) the three
Queenes meete him, and fall on their faces before him.]*

1. QUEEN.

To thee no starre be darke.

2. QUEEN.

Both heaven and earth
Friend thee for ever.

3. QUEEN.

All the good that may
Be wishd upon thy head, I cry Amen too't.

THESEUS.

Th'imparciall Gods, who from the mounted heavens
View us their mortall Heard, behold who erre,
And in their time chastice: goe and finde out
The bones of your dead Lords, and honour them
With treble Ceremonie; rather then a gap
Should be in their deere rights, we would supply't.

But those we will depute, which shall invest
You in your dignities, and even each thing
Our hast does leave imperfect: So, adiew,
And heavens good eyes looke on you. What are those? *[Exeunt Queenes.]*

HERALD.

Men of great quality, as may be judgd
By their appointment; Sone of Thebs have told's
They are Sisters children, Nephewes to the King.

THESEUS.

By'th Helme of Mars, I saw them in the war,
Like to a paire of Lions, smeard with prey,
Make lanes in troopes agast. I fixt my note
Constantly on them; for they were a marke
Worth a god's view: what prisoner was't that told me
When I enquired their names?

HERALD.

Wi'leave, they'r called Arcite and Palamon.

THESEUS.

Tis right: those, those. They are not dead?

HERALD.

Nor in a state of life: had they bin taken,
When their last hurts were given, twas possible *[3. Hearses ready.]*
They might have bin recovered; Yet they breathe
And haue the name of men.

28

THESEUS.

Then like men use 'em.
The very lees of such (millions of rates)
Exceede the wine of others: all our Surgions
Convent in their behoofe; our richest balmes
Rather then niggard, waft: their lives concerne us
Much more then Thebs is worth: rather then have 'em
Freed of this plight, and in their morning state
(Sound and at liberty) I would 'em dead;
But forty thousand fold we had rather have 'em
Prisoners to us then death. Beare 'em speedily
From our kinde aire, to them unkinde, and minister
What man to man may doe—for our sake more,
Since I have knowne frights, fury, friends beheastes,
Loves provocations, zeale, a mistris Taske,
Desire of liberty, a feavour, madnes,
Hath set a marke which nature could not reach too
Without some imposition: sicknes in will
Or wrastling strength in reason. For our Love
And great Appollos mercy, all our best
Their best skill tender. Leade into the Citty,
Where having bound things scatterd, we will post *[Florish.]*
To Athens for(e) our Army *[Exeunt. Musicke.]*

Scaena 5. (Another part of the same.)

[Enter the Queenes with the Hearses of their Knightes, in a

The Two Noble Kinsmen

Funerall Solempnity, c.]

Vrnes and odours bring away,
Vapours, sighes, darken the day;
Our dole more deadly lookes than dying;
Balmes, and Gummes, and heavy cheeres,
Sacred vials fill'd with teares,
And clamors through the wild ayre flying.

Come all sad and solempne Showes,
That are quick–eyd pleasures foes;
We convent nought else but woes.
We convent, c.

3. QUEEN.

This funeral path brings to your housholds grave:
Ioy ceaze on you againe: peace sleepe with him.

2. QUEEN.

And this to yours.

1. QUEEN.

Yours this way: Heavens lend
A thousand differing waies to one sure end.

3. QUEEN.

This world's a Citty full of straying Streetes,
And Death's the market place, where each one meetes. *[Exeunt severally.]*

Actus Secundus.

Scaena 1. (Athens. A garden, with a prison in the background.)

[Enter Iailor, and Wooer.]

IAILOR.

I may depart with little, while I live; some thing I may cast to
you, not much: Alas, the Prison I keepe, though it be for great
ones, yet they seldome come; Before one Salmon, you shall take a
number of Minnowes. I am given out to be better lyn'd then it
can appeare to me report is a true Speaker: I would I were really
that I am deliverd to be. Marry, what I have (be it what it
will)
I will assure upon my daughter at the day of my death.

WOOER.

Sir, I demaund no more then your owne offer, and I will estate
your
Daughter in what I have promised.

IAILOR.

Wel, we will talke more of this, when the solemnity is past. But
have you a full promise of her? When that shall be seene, I
tender
my consent.

[Enter Daughter.]

WOOER.

I have Sir; here shee comes.

IAILOR.

Your Friend and I have chanced to name you here, upon the old
busines: But no more of that now; so soone as the Court hurry
is over, we will have an end of it: I'th meane time looke
tenderly to the two Prisoners. I can tell you they are princes.

DAUGHTER.

These strewings are for their Chamber; tis pitty they are in
prison,
and twer pitty they should be out: I doe thinke they have
patience
to make any adversity asham'd; the prison it selfe is proud of
'em;
and they have all the world in their Chamber.

IAILOR.

They are fam'd to be a paire of absolute men.

DAUGHTER.

By my troth, I think Fame but stammers 'em; they stand a greise above the reach of report.

IAILOR.

I heard them reported in the Battaile to be the only doers.

DAUGHTER.

Nay, most likely, for they are noble suffrers; I mervaile how
they
would have lookd had they beene Victors, that with such a
constant
Nobility enforce a freedome out of Bondage, making misery their
Mirth,
and affliction a toy to jest at.

IAILOR.

Doe they so?

DAUGHTER.

It seemes to me they have no more sence of their Captivity, then
I
of ruling Athens: they eate well, looke merrily, discourse of
many
things, but nothing of their owne restraint, and disasters: yet
sometime a devided sigh, martyrd as 'twer i'th deliverance, will
breake from one of them; when the other presently gives it so
sweete
a rebuke, that I could wish my selfe a Sigh to be so chid, or at
least a Sigher to be comforted.

WOOER.

I never saw 'em.

IAILOR.

The Duke himselfe came privately in the night,

[Enter Palamon, and Arcite, above.]

and so did they: what the reason of it is, I know not: Looke, yonder
they are! that's Arcite lookes out.

DAUGHTER.

No, Sir, no, that's Palamon: Arcite is the lower of the twaine; you
may perceive a part of him.

IAILOR.

Goe too, leave your pointing; they would not make us their object;
out of their sight.

DAUGHTER.

It is a holliday to looke on them: Lord, the diffrence of men!
[Exeunt.]

Scaena 2. (The prison)

[Enter Palamon, and Arcite in prison.]

PALAMON.

How doe you, Noble Cosen?

ARCITE.

How doe you, Sir?

PALAMON.

Why strong inough to laugh at misery,
And beare the chance of warre, yet we are prisoners,
I feare, for ever, Cosen.

ARCITE.

I beleeve it,
And to that destiny have patiently
Laide up my houre to come.

PALAMON.

O Cosen Arcite,
Where is Thebs now? where is our noble Country?
Where are our friends, and kindreds? never more
Must we behold those comforts, never see
The hardy youthes strive for the Games of honour
(Hung with the painted favours of their Ladies,
Like tall Ships under saile) then start among'st 'em
And as an Eastwind leave 'en all behinde us,
Like lazy Clowdes, whilst Palamon and Arcite,
Even in the wagging of a wanton leg
Out–stript the peoples praises, won the Garlands,

Ere they have time to wish 'em ours. O never
Shall we two exercise, like Twyns of honour,
Our Armes againe, and feele our fyry horses
Like proud Seas under us: our good Swords now
(Better the red—eyd god of war nev'r wore)
Ravishd our sides, like age must run to rust,
And decke the Temples of those gods that hate us:
These hands shall never draw'em out like lightning,
To blast whole Armies more.

ARCITE.

No, Palamon,
Those hopes are Prisoners with us; here we are
And here the graces of our youthes must wither
Like a too—timely Spring; here age must finde us,
And, which is heaviest, Palamon, unmarried;
The sweete embraces of a loving wife,
Loden with kisses, armd with thousand Cupids
Shall never claspe our neckes, no issue know us,
No figures of our selves shall we ev'r see,
To glad our age, and like young Eagles teach 'em
Boldly to gaze against bright armes, and say:
'Remember what your fathers were, and conquer.'
The faire—eyd Maides, shall weepe our Banishments,
And in their Songs, curse ever—blinded fortune,
Till shee for shame see what a wrong she has done
To youth and nature. This is all our world;
We shall know nothing here but one another,
Heare nothing but the Clocke that tels our woes.
The Vine shall grow, but we shall never see it:
Sommer shall come, and with her all delights;
But dead—cold winter must inhabite here still.

PALAMON.

36

Tis too true, Arcite. To our Theban houndes,
That shooke the aged Forrest with their ecchoes,
No more now must we halloa, no more shake
Our pointed Iavelyns, whilst the angry Swine
Flyes like a parthian quiver from our rages,
Strucke with our well–steeld Darts: All valiant uses
(The foode, and nourishment of noble mindes,)
In us two here shall perish; we shall die
(Which is the curse of honour) lastly
Children of greife, and Ignorance.

ARCITE.

Yet, Cosen,
Even from the bottom of these miseries,
From all that fortune can inflict upon us,
I see two comforts rysing, two meere blessings,
If the gods please: to hold here a brave patience,
And the enjoying of our greefes together.
Whilst Palamon is with me, let me perish
If I thinke this our prison.

PALAMON.

Certeinly,
Tis a maine goodnes, Cosen, that our fortunes
Were twyn'd together; tis most true, two soules
Put in two noble Bodies—let 'em suffer
The gaule of hazard, so they grow together—
Will never sincke; they must not, say they could:
A willing man dies sleeping, and all's done.

ARCITE.

Shall we make worthy uses of this place
That all men hate so much?

PALAMON.

How, gentle Cosen?

ARCITE.

Let's thinke this prison holy sanctuary,
To keepe us from corruption of worse men.
We are young and yet desire the waies of honour,
That liberty and common Conversation,
The poyson of pure spirits, might like women
Wooe us to wander from. What worthy blessing
Can be but our Imaginations
May make it ours? And heere being thus together,
We are an endles mine to one another;
We are one anothers wife, ever begetting
New birthes of love; we are father, friends, acquaintance;
We are, in one another, Families,
I am your heire, and you are mine: This place
Is our Inheritance, no hard Oppressour
Dare take this from us; here, with a little patience,
We shall live long, and loving: No surfeits seeke us:
The hand of war hurts none here, nor the Seas
Swallow their youth: were we at liberty,
A wife might part us lawfully, or busines;
Quarrels consume us, Envy of ill men
Grave our acquaintance; I might sicken, Cosen,
Where you should never know it, and so perish
Without your noble hand to close mine eies,
Or praiers to the gods: a thousand chaunces,
Were we from hence, would seaver us.

PALAMON.

You have made me

(I thanke you, Cosen Arcite) almost wanton
With my Captivity: what a misery
It is to live abroade, and every where!
Tis like a Beast, me thinkes: I finde the Court here—
I am sure, a more content; and all those pleasures
That wooe the wils of men to vanity,
I see through now, and am sufficient
To tell the world, tis but a gaudy shaddow,
That old Time, as he passes by, takes with him.
What had we bin, old in the Court of Creon,
Where sin is Iustice, lust and ignorance
The vertues of the great ones! Cosen Arcite,
Had not the loving gods found this place for us,
We had died as they doe, ill old men, unwept,
And had their Epitaphes, the peoples Curses:
Shall I say more?

ARCITE.

I would heare you still.

PALAMON.

Ye shall.
Is there record of any two that lov'd
Better then we doe, Arcite?

ARCITE.

Sure, there cannot.

PALAMON.

I doe not thinke it possible our friendship
Should ever leave us.

ARCITE.

Till our deathes it cannot;

[Enter Emilia and her woman (below).]

And after death our spirits shall be led
To those that love eternally. Speake on, Sir.

EMILIA.

This garden has a world of pleasures in't.
What Flowre is this?

WOMAN.

Tis calld Narcissus, Madam.

EMILIA.

That was a faire Boy, certaine, but a foole,
To love himselfe; were there not maides enough?

ARCITE.

Pray forward.

PALAMON.

Yes.

EMILIA.

Or were they all hard hearted?

WOMAN.

They could not be to one so faire.

EMILIA.

Thou wouldst not.

WOMAN.

I thinke I should not, Madam.

EMILIA.

That's a good wench:
But take heede to your kindnes though.

WOMAN.

Why, Madam?

EMILIA.

Men are mad things.

ARCITE.

Will ye goe forward, Cosen?

EMILIA.

Canst not thou worke such flowers in silke, wench?

WOMAN.

Yes.

EMILIA.

Ile have a gowne full of 'em, and of these;
This is a pretty colour, wilt not doe
Rarely upon a Skirt, wench?

WOMAN.

Deinty, Madam.

ARCITE.

Cosen, Cosen, how doe you, Sir? Why, Palamon?

PALAMON.

Never till now I was in prison, Arcite.

ARCITE.

Why whats the matter, Man?

PALAMON.

Behold, and wonder.
By heaven, shee is a Goddesse.

ARCITE.

Ha.

PALAMON.

Doe reverence. She is a Goddesse, Arcite.

EMILIA.

Of all Flowres, me thinkes a Rose is best.

WOMAN.

Why, gentle Madam?

EMILIA.

It is the very Embleme of a Maide.
For when the west wind courts her gently,
How modestly she blowes, and paints the Sun,
With her chaste blushes! When the North comes neere her,
Rude and impatient, then, like Chastity,
Shee lockes her beauties in her bud againe,
And leaves him to base briers.

WOMAN.

Yet, good Madam,
Sometimes her modesty will blow so far
She fals for't: a Mayde,
If shee have any honour, would be loth
To take example by her.

EMILIA.

Thou art wanton.

ARCITE.

She is wondrous faire.

PALAMON.

She is beauty extant.

EMILIA.

The Sun grows high, lets walk in: keep these flowers;
Weele see how neere Art can come neere their colours.
I am wondrous merry hearted, I could laugh now.

WOMAN.

I could lie downe, I am sure.

EMILIA.

And take one with you?

WOMAN.

That's as we bargaine, Madam.

EMILIA.

Well, agree then. *[Exeunt Emilia and woman.]*

PALAMON.

What thinke you of this beauty?

ARCITE.

Tis a rare one.

PALAMON.

Is't but a rare one?

ARCITE.

Yes, a matchles beauty.

PALAMON.

Might not a man well lose himselfe and love her?

ARCITE.

I cannot tell what you have done, I have;
Beshrew mine eyes for't: now I feele my Shackles.

PALAMON.

You love her, then?

ARCITE.

Who would not?

PALAMON.

And desire her?

ARCITE.

Before my liberty.

PALAMON.

I saw her first.

ARCITE.

That's nothing.

PALAMON.

But it shall be.

ARCITE.

I saw her too.

PALAMON.

Yes, but you must not love her.

ARCITE.

I will not as you doe, to worship her,
As she is heavenly, and a blessed Goddes;
I love her as a woman, to enjoy her:
So both may love.

PALAMON.

You shall not love at all.

ARCITE.

Not love at all!
Who shall deny me?

PALAMON.

I, that first saw her; I, that tooke possession
First with mine eyes of all those beauties
In her reveald to mankinde: if thou lou'st her,
Or entertain'st a hope to blast my wishes,
Thou art a Traytour, Arcite, and a fellow
False as thy Title to her: friendship, blood,

And all the tyes betweene us I disclaime,
If thou once thinke upon her.

ARCITE.

Yes, I love her,
And if the lives of all my name lay on it,
I must doe so; I love her with my soule:
If that will lose ye, farewell, Palamon;
I say againe, I love, and in loving her maintaine
I am as worthy and as free a lover,
And have as just a title to her beauty
As any Palamon or any living
That is a mans Sonne.

PALAMON.

Have I cald thee friend?

ARCITE.

Yes, and have found me so; why are you mov'd thus?
Let me deale coldly with you: am not I
Part of your blood, part of your soule? you have told me
That I was Palamon, and you were Arcite.

PALAMON.

Yes.

ARCITE.

Am not I liable to those affections,
Those joyes, greifes, angers, feares, my friend shall suffer?

PALAMON.

Ye may be.

ARCITE.

Why, then, would you deale so cunningly,
So strangely, so vnlike a noble kinesman,
To love alone? speake truely: doe you thinke me
Vnworthy of her sight?

PALAMON.

No; but unjust,
If thou pursue that sight.

ARCITE.

Because an other
First sees the Enemy, shall I stand still
And let mine honour downe, and never charge?

PALAMON.

Yes, if he be but one.

ARCITE.

But say that one
Had rather combat me?

PALAMON.

Let that one say so,
And use thy freedome; els if thou pursuest her,
Be as that cursed man that hates his Country,
A branded villaine.

ARCITE.

You are mad.

PALAMON.

I must be,
Till thou art worthy, Arcite; it concernes me,
And in this madnes, if I hazard thee
And take thy life, I deale but truely.

ARCITE.

Fie, Sir,
You play the Childe extreamely: I will love her,
I must, I ought to doe so, and I dare;
And all this justly.

PALAMON.

O that now, that now
Thy false—selfe and thy friend had but this fortune,
To be one howre at liberty, and graspe
Our good Swords in our hands! I would quickly teach thee
What 'twer to filch affection from another:
Thou art baser in it then a Cutpurse;
Put but thy head out of this window more,
And as I have a soule, Ile naile thy life too't.

ARCITE.

Thou dar'st not, foole, thou canst not, thou art feeble.
Put my head out? Ile throw my Body out,
And leape the garden, when I see her next

[Enter Keeper.]

And pitch between her armes to anger thee.

PALAMON.

No more; the keeper's comming; I shall live
To knocke thy braines out with my Shackles.

ARCITE.

Doe.

KEEPER.

By your leave, Gentlemen—

PALAMON.

Now, honest keeper?

KEEPER.

Lord Arcite, you must presently to'th Duke;
The cause I know not yet.

ARCITE.

I am ready, keeper.

KEEPER.

Prince Palamon, I must awhile bereave you
Of your faire Cosens Company. *[Exeunt Arcite, and Keeper.]*

PALAMON.

And me too,
Even when you please, of life. Why is he sent for?
It may be he shall marry her; he's goodly,
And like enough the Duke hath taken notice
Both of his blood and body: But his falsehood!
Why should a friend be treacherous? If that
Get him a wife so noble, and so faire,
Let honest men ne're love againe. Once more
I would but see this faire One. Blessed Garden,
And fruite, and flowers more blessed, that still blossom
As her bright eies shine on ye! would I were,
For all the fortune of my life hereafter,
Yon little Tree, yon blooming Apricocke;
How I would spread, and fling my wanton armes
In at her window; I would bring her fruite
Fit for the Gods to feed on: youth and pleasure
Still as she tasted should be doubled on her,
And if she be not heavenly, I would make her
So neere the Gods in nature, they should feare her,

[Enter Keeper.]

And then I am sure she would love me. How now, keeper.
Wher's Arcite?

KEEPER.

Banishd: Prince Pirithous
Obtained his liberty; but never more
Vpon his oth and life must he set foote
Vpon this Kingdome.

PALAMON.

Hees a blessed man!

51

He shall see Thebs againe, and call to Armes
The bold yong men, that, when he bids 'em charge,
Fall on like fire: Arcite shall have a Fortune,
If he dare make himselfe a worthy Lover,
Yet in the Feild to strike a battle for her;
And if he lose her then, he's a cold Coward;
How bravely may he beare himselfe to win her
If he be noble Arcite—thousand waies.
Were I at liberty, I would doe things
Of such a vertuous greatnes, that this Lady,
This blushing virgine, should take manhood to her
And seeke to ravish me.

KEEPER.

My Lord for you
I have this charge too—

PALAMON.

To discharge my life?

KEEPER.

No, but from this place to remoove your Lordship:
The windowes are too open.

PALAMON.

Devils take 'em,
That are so envious to me! pre'thee kill me.

KEEPER.

And hang for't afterward.

PALAMON.

By this good light,
Had I a sword I would kill thee.

KEEPER.

Why, my Lord?

PALAMON.

Thou bringst such pelting scuruy news continually
Thou art not worthy life. I will not goe.

KEEPER.

Indeede, you must, my Lord.

PALAMON.

May I see the garden?

KEEPER.

Noe.

PALAMON.

Then I am resolud, I will not goe.

KEEPER.

I must constraine you then: and for you are dangerous,
Ile clap more yrons on you.

PALAMON.

Doe, good keeper.
Ile shake 'em so, ye shall not sleepe;
Ile make ye a new Morrisse: must I goe?

KEEPER.

There is no remedy.

PALAMON.

Farewell, kinde window.
May rude winde never hurt thee. O, my Lady,
If ever thou hast felt what sorrow was,
Dreame how I suffer. Come; now bury me. *[Exeunt Palamon, and
Keeper.]*

Scaena 3. (The country near Athens.)

[Enter Arcite.]

ARCITE.

Banishd the kingdome? tis a benefit,
A mercy I must thanke 'em for, but banishd
The free enjoying of that face I die for,
Oh twas a studdied punishment, a death
Beyond Imagination: Such a vengeance
That, were I old and wicked, all my sins

Could never plucke upon me. Palamon,
Thou ha'st the Start now, thou shalt stay and see
Her bright eyes breake each morning gainst thy window,
And let in life into thee; thou shalt feede
Vpon the sweetenes of a noble beauty,
That nature nev'r exceeded, nor nev'r shall:
Good gods! what happines has Palamon!
Twenty to one, hee'le come to speake to her,
And if she be as gentle as she's faire,
I know she's his; he has a Tongue will tame
Tempests, and make the wild Rockes wanton.
Come what can come,
The worst is death; I will not leave the Kingdome.
I know mine owne is but a heape of ruins,
And no redresse there; if I goe, he has her.
I am resolu'd an other shape shall make me,
Or end my fortunes. Either way, I am happy:
Ile see her, and be neere her, or no more.

[Enter 4. Country people, one with a garlond before them.]

1. COUNTREYMAN

My Masters, ile be there, that's certaine

2. COUNTREYMAN

And Ile be there.

3. COUNTREYMAN

And I.

4. COUNTREYMAN

Why, then, have with ye, Boyes; Tis but a chiding.

Let the plough play to day, ile tick'lt out
Of the Iades tailes to morrow.

1. COUNTREYMAN

I am sure
To have my wife as jealous as a Turkey:
But that's all one; ile goe through, let her mumble.

2. COUNTREYMAN

Clap her aboard to morrow night, and stoa her,
And all's made up againe.

3. COUNTREYMAN

I, doe but put a feskue in her fist, and you shall see her
Take a new lesson out, and be a good wench.
Doe we all hold against the Maying?

4. COUNTREYMAN

Hold? what should aile us?

3. COUNTREYMAN

Arcas will be there.

2. COUNTREYMAN

And Sennois.
And Rycas, and 3. better lads nev'r dancd
Under green Tree. And yee know what wenches: ha?
But will the dainty Domine, the Schoolemaster,
Keep touch, doe you thinke? for he do's all, ye know.

3. COUNTREYMAN

Hee'l eate a hornebooke ere he faile: goe too, the matter's too
farre driven betweene him and the Tanners daughter, to let slip
now, and she must see the Duke, and she must daunce too.

4. COUNTREYMAN

Shall we be lusty?

2. COUNTREYMAN

All the Boyes in Athens blow wind i'th breech on's, and heere ile
be and there ile be, for our Towne, and here againe, and there
againe:
ha, Boyes, heigh for the weavers.

1. COUNTREYMAN

This must be done i'th woods.

4. COUNTREYMAN

O, pardon me.

2. COUNTREYMAN

By any meanes, our thing of learning saies so:
Where he himselfe will edifie the Duke
Most parlously in our behalfes: hees excellent i'th woods;
Bring him to'th plaines, his learning makes no cry.

3. COUNTREYMAN

Weele see the sports, then; every man to's Tackle:
And, Sweete Companions, lets rehearse by any meanes,

Before the Ladies see us, and doe sweetly,
And God knows what May come on't.

4. COUNTREYMAN

Content; the sports once ended, wee'l performe.
Away, Boyes and hold.

ARCITE.

By your leaves, honest friends: pray you, whither goe you?

4. COUNTREYMAN

Whither? why, what a question's that?

ARCITE.

Yes, tis a question, to me that know not.

3. COUNTREYMAN

To the Games, my Friend.

2. COUNTREYMAN

Where were you bred, you know it not?

ARCITE.

Not farre, Sir,
Are there such Games to day?

1. COUNTREYMAN

Yes, marry, are there:

And so would any young wench, o' my Conscience,
That ever dream'd, or vow'd her Maydenhead
To a yong hansom Man; Then I lov'd him,
Extreamely lov'd him, infinitely lov'd him;
And yet he had a Cosen, faire as he too.
But in my heart was Palamon, and there,
Lord, what a coyle he keepes! To heare him
Sing in an evening, what a heaven it is!
And yet his Songs are sad ones. Fairer spoken
Was never Gentleman. When I come in
To bring him water in a morning, first
He bowes his noble body, then salutes me, thus:
'Faire, gentle Mayde, good morrow; may thy goodnes
Get thee a happy husband.' Once he kist me.
I lov'd my lips the better ten daies after.
Would he would doe so ev'ry day! He greives much,
And me as much to see his misery.
What should I doe, to make him know I love him?
For I would faine enjoy him. Say I ventur'd
To set him free? what saies the law then? Thus much
For Law, or kindred! I will doe it,
And this night, or to morrow, he shall love me. *[Exit.]*

Scaena 5. (An open place in Athens.)

[Enter Theseus, Hipolita, Pirithous, Emilia: Arcite with a Garland, c.]

[This short florish of Cornets and Showtes within.]

61

The Two Noble Kinsmen

THESEUS.

You have done worthily; I have not seene,
Since Hercules, a man of tougher synewes;
What ere you are, you run the best, and wrastle,
That these times can allow.

ARCITE.

I am proud to please you.

THESEUS.

What Countrie bred you?

ARCITE.

This; but far off, Prince.

THESEUS.

Are you a Gentleman?

ARCITE.

My father said so;
And to those gentle uses gave me life.

THESEUS.

Are you his heire?

ARCITE.

His yongest, Sir.

THESEUS.

Your Father
Sure is a happy Sire then: what prooves you?

ARCITE.

A little of all noble Quallities:
I could have kept a Hawke, and well have holloa'd
To a deepe crie of Dogges; I dare not praise
My feat in horsemanship, yet they that knew me
Would say it was my best peece: last, and greatest,
I would be thought a Souldier.

THESEUS.

You are perfect.

PERITHOUS.

Vpon my soule, a proper man.

EMILIA.

He is so.

PERITHOUS.

How doe you like him, Ladie?

HIPPOLITA.

I admire him;
I have not seene so yong a man so noble
(If he say true,) of his sort.

EMILIA.

Beleeve,
His mother was a wondrous handsome woman;
His face, me thinkes, goes that way.

HIPPOLITA.

But his Body
And firie minde illustrate a brave Father.

PERITHOUS.

Marke how his vertue, like a hidden Sun,
Breakes through his baser garments.

HIPPOLITA.

Hee's well got, sure.

THESEUS.

What made you seeke this place, Sir?

ARCITE.

Noble Theseus,
To purchase name, and doe my ablest service
To such a well–found wonder as thy worth,
For onely in thy Court, of all the world,
Dwells faire–eyd honor.

PERITHOUS.

All his words are worthy.

THESEUS.

Sir, we are much endebted to your travell,
Nor shall you loose your wish: Perithous,
Dispose of this faire Gentleman.

PERITHOUS.

Thankes, Theseus.
What ere you are y'ar mine, and I shall give you
To a most noble service, to this Lady,
This bright yong Virgin; pray, observe her goodnesse;
You have honourd hir faire birth–day with your vertues,
And as your due y'ar hirs: kisse her faire hand, Sir.

ARCITE.

Sir, y'ar a noble Giver: dearest Bewtie,
Thus let me seale my vowd faith: when your Servant
(Your most unworthie Creature) but offends you,
Command him die, he shall.

EMILIA.

That were too cruell.
If you deserve well, Sir, I shall soone see't:
Y'ar mine, and somewhat better than your rancke
Ile use you.

PERITHOUS.

Ile see you furnish'd, and because you say
You are a horseman, I must needs intreat you
This after noone to ride, but tis a rough one.

ARCITE.

I like him better, Prince, I shall not then
Freeze in my Saddle.

THESEUS.

Sweet, you must be readie,
And you, Emilia, and you, Friend, and all,
To morrow by the Sun, to doe observance
To flowry May, in Dians wood: waite well, Sir,
Vpon your Mistris. Emely, I hope
He shall not goe a foote.

EMILIA.

That were a shame, Sir,
While I have horses: take your choice, and what
You want at any time, let me but know it;
If you serve faithfully, I dare assure you
You'l finde a loving Mistris.

ARCITE.

If I doe not,
Let me finde that my Father ever hated,
Disgrace and blowes.

THESEUS.

Go, leade the way; you have won it:
It shall be so; you shall receave all dues
Fit for the honour you have won; Twer wrong else.
Sister, beshrew my heart, you have a Servant,
That, if I were a woman, would be Master,
But you are wise. *[Florish.]*

EMILIA.

I hope too wise for that, Sir. *[Exeunt omnes.]*

Scaena 6. (Before the prison.)

[Enter Iaylors Daughter alone.]

DAUGHTER.

Let all the Dukes, and all the divells rore,
He is at liberty: I have venturd for him,
And out I have brought him to a little wood
A mile hence. I have sent him, where a Cedar,
Higher than all the rest, spreads like a plane
Fast by a Brooke, and there he shall keepe close,
Till I provide him Fyles and foode, for yet
His yron bracelets are not off. O Love,
What a stout hearted child thou art! My Father
Durst better have indur'd cold yron, than done it:
I love him beyond love and beyond reason,
Or wit, or safetie: I have made him know it.
I care not, I am desperate; If the law
Finde me, and then condemne me for't, some wenches,
Some honest harted Maides, will sing my Dirge,
And tell to memory my death was noble,
Dying almost a Martyr: That way he takes,
I purpose is my way too: Sure he cannot

Be so unmanly, as to leave me here;
If he doe, Maides will not so easily
Trust men againe: And yet he has not thank'd me
For what I have done: no not so much as kist me,
And that (me thinkes) is not so well; nor scarcely
Could I perswade him to become a Freeman,
He made such scruples of the wrong he did
To me, and to my Father. Yet I hope,
When he considers more, this love of mine
Will take more root within him: Let him doe
What he will with me, so he use me kindly;
For use me so he shall, or ile proclaime him,
And to his face, no man. Ile presently
Provide him necessaries, and packe my cloathes up,
And where there is a patch of ground Ile venture,
So hee be with me; By him, like a shadow,
Ile ever dwell; within this houre the whoobub
Will be all ore the prison: I am then
Kissing the man they looke for: farewell, Father;
Get many more such prisoners and such daughters,
And shortly you may keepe your selfe. Now to him!

Actus Tertius.

Scaena 1. (A forest near Athens.)

[Cornets in sundry places. Noise and hallowing as people a Maying.]

[Enter Arcite alone.]

ARCITE.

The Duke has lost Hypolita; each tooke
A severall land. This is a solemne Right
They owe bloomd May, and the Athenians pay it
To'th heart of Ceremony. O Queene Emilia,
Fresher then May, sweeter
Then hir gold Buttons on the bowes, or all
Th'enamelld knackes o'th Meade or garden: yea,
We challenge too the bancke of any Nymph
That makes the streame seeme flowers; thou, o Iewell
O'th wood, o'th world, hast likewise blest a place
With thy sole presence: in thy rumination
That I, poore man, might eftsoones come betweene
And chop on some cold thought! thrice blessed chance,
To drop on such a Mistris, expectation
Most giltlesse on't! tell me, O Lady Fortune,
(Next after Emely my Soveraigne) how far
I may be prowd. She takes strong note of me,
Hath made me neere her; and this beuteous Morne
(The prim'st of all the yeare) presents me with
A brace of horses: two such Steeds might well
Be by a paire of Kings backt, in a Field
That their crownes titles tride. Alas, alas,
Poore Cosen Palamon, poore prisoner, thou
So little dream'st upon my fortune, that

Thou thinkst thy selfe the happier thing, to be
So neare Emilia; me thou deem'st at Thebs,
And therein wretched, although free. But if
Thou knew'st my Mistris breathd on me, and that
I ear'd her language, livde in her eye, O Coz,
What passion would enclose thee!

*[Enter Palamon as out of a Bush, with his Shackles: bends his fist
at Arcite.]*

PALAMON.

Traytor kinesman,
Thou shouldst perceive my passion, if these signes
Of prisonment were off me, and this hand
But owner of a Sword: By all othes in one,
I and the iustice of my love would make thee
A confest Traytor. O thou most perfidious
That ever gently lookd; the voydest of honour,
That eu'r bore gentle Token; falsest Cosen
That ever blood made kin, call'st thou hir thine?
Ile prove it in my Shackles, with these hands,
Void of appointment, that thou ly'st, and art
A very theefe in love, a Chaffy Lord,
Nor worth the name of villaine: had I a Sword
And these house clogges away—

ARCITE.

Deere Cosin Palamon—

PALAMON.

Cosoner Arcite, give me language such
As thou hast shewd me feate.

ARCITE.

Not finding in
The circuit of my breast any grosse stuffe
To forme me like your blazon, holds me to
This gentlenesse of answer; tis your passion
That thus mistakes, the which to you being enemy,
Cannot to me be kind: honor, and honestie
I cherish, and depend on, how so ev'r
You skip them in me, and with them, faire Coz,
Ile maintaine my proceedings; pray, be pleas'd
To shew in generous termes your griefes, since that
Your question's with your equall, who professes
To cleare his owne way with the minde and Sword
Of a true Gentleman.

PALAMON.

That thou durst, Arcite!

ARCITE.

My Coz, my Coz, you have beene well advertis'd
How much I dare, y'ave seene me use my Sword
Against th'advice of feare: sure, of another
You would not heare me doubted, but your silence
Should breake out, though i'th Sanctuary.

PALAMON.

Sir,
I have seene you move in such a place, which well
Might justifie your manhood; you were calld
A good knight and a bold; But the whole weeke's not faire,
If any day it rayne: Their valiant temper

Men loose when they encline to trecherie,
And then they fight like coupelld Beares, would fly
Were they not tyde.

ARCITE.

Kinsman, you might as well
Speake this and act it in your Glasse, as to
His eare which now disdaines you.

PALAMON.

Come up to me,
Quit me of these cold Gyves, give me a Sword,
Though it be rustie, and the charity
Of one meale lend me; Come before me then,
A good Sword in thy hand, and doe but say
That Emily is thine: I will forgive
The trespasse thou hast done me, yea, my life,
If then thou carry't, and brave soules in shades
That have dyde manly, which will seeke of me
Some newes from earth, they shall get none but this,
That thou art brave and noble.

ARCITE.

Be content:
Againe betake you to your hawthorne house;
With counsaile of the night, I will be here
With wholesome viands; these impediments
Will I file off; you shall have garments and
Perfumes to kill the smell o'th prison; after,
When you shall stretch your selfe and say but, 'Arcite,
I am in plight,' there shall be at your choyce
Both Sword and Armour.

PALAMON.

Oh you heavens, dares any
So noble beare a guilty busines! none
But onely Arcite, therefore none but Arcite
In this kinde is so bold.

ARCITE.

Sweete Palamon.

PALAMON.

I doe embrace you and your offer,—for
Your offer doo't I onely, Sir; your person,
Without hipocrisy I may not wish *[Winde hornes of Cornets.]*
More then my Swords edge ont.

ARCITE.

You heare the Hornes;
Enter your Musite least this match between's
Be crost, er met: give me your hand; farewell.
Ile bring you every needfull thing: I pray you,
Take comfort and be strong.

PALAMON.

Pray hold your promise;
And doe the deede with a bent brow: most certaine
You love me not, be rough with me, and powre
This oile out of your language; by this ayre,
I could for each word give a Cuffe, my stomach
Not reconcild by reason.

ARCITE.

Plainely spoken,
Yet pardon me hard language: when I spur *[Winde hornes.]*
My horse, I chide him not; content and anger
In me have but one face. Harke, Sir, they call
The scatterd to the Banket; you must guesse
I have an office there.

PALAMON.

Sir, your attendance
Cannot please heaven, and I know your office
Vnjustly is atcheev'd.

ARCITE.

If a good title,
I am perswaded this question sicke between's
By bleeding must be cur'd. I am a Suitour,
That to your Sword you will bequeath this plea
And talke of it no more.

PALAMON.

But this one word:
You are going now to gaze upon my Mistris,
For note you, mine she is—

ARCITE.

Nay, then.

PALAMON.

Nay, pray you,
You talke of feeding me to breed me strength:

74

You are going now to looke upon a Sun
That strengthens what it lookes on; there
You have a vantage ore me, but enjoy't till
I may enforce my remedy. Farewell. *[Exeunt.]*

Scaena 2. (Another Part of the forest.)

[Enter Iaylors daughter alone.]

DAUGHTER.

He has mistooke the Brake I meant, is gone
After his fancy. Tis now welnigh morning;
No matter, would it were perpetuall night,
And darkenes Lord o'th world. Harke, tis a woolfe:
In me hath greife slaine feare, and but for one thing
I care for nothing, and that's Palamon.
I wreake not if the wolves would jaw me, so
He had this File: what if I hallowd for him?
I cannot hallow: if I whoop'd, what then?
If he not answeard, I should call a wolfe,
And doe him but that service. I have heard
Strange howles this live—long night, why may't not be
They have made prey of him? he has no weapons,
He cannot run, the Iengling of his Gives
Might call fell things to listen, who have in them
A sence to know a man unarmd, and can
Smell where resistance is. Ile set it downe
He's torne to peeces; they howld many together

And then they fed on him: So much for that,
Be bold to ring the Bell; how stand I then?
All's char'd when he is gone. No, no, I lye,
My Father's to be hang'd for his escape;
My selfe to beg, if I prizd life so much
As to deny my act, but that I would not,
Should I try death by dussons.—I am mop't,
Food tooke I none these two daies,
Sipt some water. I have not closd mine eyes
Save when my lids scowrd off their brine; alas,
Dissolue my life, Let not my sence unsettle,
Least I should drowne, or stab or hang my selfe.
O state of Nature, faile together in me,
Since thy best props are warpt! So, which way now?
The best way is the next way to a grave:
Each errant step beside is torment. Loe,
The Moone is down, the Cryckets chirpe, the Schreichowle
Calls in the dawne; all offices are done
Save what I faile in: But the point is this,
An end, and that is all. *[Exit.]*

Scaena 3. (Same as Scene I.)

[Enter Arcite, with Meate, Wine, and Files.]

ARCITE.

I should be neere the place: hoa, Cosen Palamon. *[Enter Palamon.]*

PALAMON.

Arcite?

ARCITE.

The same: I have brought you foode and files.
Come forth and feare not, here's no Theseus.

PALAMON.

Nor none so honest, Arcite.

ARCITE.

That's no matter,
Wee'l argue that hereafter: Come, take courage;
You shall not dye thus beastly: here, Sir, drinke;
I know you are faint: then ile talke further with you.

PALAMON.

Arcite, thou mightst now poyson me.

ARCITE.

I might,
But I must feare you first: Sit downe, and, good, now
No more of these vaine parlies; let us not,
Having our ancient reputation with us,
Make talke for Fooles and Cowards. To your health, c.

PALAMON.

Doe.

ARCITE.

Pray, sit downe then; and let me entreate you,
By all the honesty and honour in you,
No mention of this woman: t'will disturbe us;
We shall have time enough.

PALAMON.

Well, Sir, Ile pledge you.

ARCITE.

Drinke a good hearty draught; it breeds good blood, man.
Doe not you feele it thaw you?

PALAMON.

Stay, Ile tell you after a draught or two more.

ARCITE.

Spare it not, the Duke has more, Cuz: Eate now.

PALAMON.

Yes.

ARCITE.

I am glad you have so good a stomach.

PALAMON.

I am gladder I have so good meate too't.

ARCITE.

Is't not mad lodging here in the wild woods, Cosen?

PALAMON.

Yes, for them that have wilde Consciences.

ARCITE.

How tasts your vittails? your hunger needs no sawce, I see.

PALAMON.

Not much;
But if it did, yours is too tart, sweete Cosen: what is this?

ARCITE.

Venison.

PALAMON.

Tis a lusty meate:
Giue me more wine; here, Arcite, to the wenches
We have known in our daies. The Lord Stewards daughter,
Doe you remember her?

ARCITE.

After you, Cuz.

PALAMON.

She lov'd a black–haird man.

ARCITE.

She did so; well, Sir.

PALAMON.

And I have heard some call him Arcite, and—

ARCITE.

Out with't, faith.

PALAMON.

She met him in an Arbour:
What did she there, Cuz? play o'th virginals?

ARCITE.

Something she did, Sir.

PALAMON.

Made her groane a moneth for't, or 2. or 3. or 10.

ARCITE.

The Marshals Sister
Had her share too, as I remember, Cosen,
Else there be tales abroade; you'l pledge her?

PALAMON.

Yes.

ARCITE.

A pretty broune wench t'is. There was a time
When yong men went a hunting, and a wood,
And a broade Beech: and thereby hangs a tale:—heigh ho!

PALAMON.

For Emily, upon my life! Foole,
Away with this straind mirth; I say againe,
That sigh was breathd for Emily; base Cosen,
Dar'st thou breake first?

ARCITE.

You are wide.

PALAMON.

By heaven and earth, ther's nothing in thee honest.

ARCITE.

Then Ile leave you: you are a Beast now.

PALAMON.

As thou makst me, Traytour.

ARCITE.

Ther's all things needfull, files and shirts, and perfumes:
Ile come againe some two howres hence, and bring
That that shall quiet all,

PALAMON.

A Sword and Armour?

ARCITE.

Feare me not; you are now too fowle; farewell.
Get off your Trinkets; you shall want nought.

PALAMON.

Sir, ha—

ARCITE.

Ile heare no more. *[Exit.]*

PALAMON.

If he keepe touch, he dies for't. *[Exit.]*

Scaena 4. (Another part of the forest.)

[Enter Iaylors daughter.]

DAUGHTER.

I am very cold, and all the Stars are out too,
The little Stars, and all, that looke like aglets:
The Sun has seene my Folly. Palamon!

Alas no; hees in heaven. Where am I now?
Yonder's the sea, and ther's a Ship; how't tumbles!
And ther's a Rocke lies watching under water;
Now, now, it beates upon it; now, now, now,
Ther's a leak sprung, a sound one, how they cry!
Spoon her before the winde, you'l loose all els:
Vp with a course or two, and take about, Boyes.
Good night, good night, y'ar gone.—I am very hungry.
Would I could finde a fine Frog; he would tell me
Newes from all parts o'th world, then would I make
A Carecke of a Cockle shell, and sayle
By east and North East to the King of Pigmes,
For he tels fortunes rarely. Now my Father,
Twenty to one, is trust up in a trice
To morrow morning; Ile say never a word.

[Sing.]

For ile cut my greene coat a foote above my knee,
And ile clip my yellow lockes an inch below mine eie.
hey, nonny, nonny, nonny,
He's buy me a white Cut, forth for to ride
And ile goe seeke him, throw the world that is so wide
hey nonny, nonny, nonny.

O for a pricke now like a Nightingale,
To put my breast against. I shall sleepe like a Top else.
[Exit.]

Scaena 5. (Another part of the forest.)

[Enter a Schoole master, 4. Countrymen, and Bavian. 2. or 3. wenches,
with a Taborer.]

SCHOOLMASTER.

Fy, fy, what tediosity, disensanity is here among ye? have
my Rudiments bin labourd so long with ye? milkd unto ye, and
by a figure even the very plumbroth marrow of my understanding
laid upon ye? and do you still cry: where, and how, wherfore?
you most course freeze capacities, ye jane Iudgements, have I
saide:
thus let be, and there let be, and then let be, and no man
understand
mee? Proh deum, medius fidius, ye are all dunces! For why, here
stand I, Here the Duke comes, there are you close in the Thicket;
the Duke appeares, I meete him and unto him I utter learned
things
and many figures; he heares, and nods, and hums, and then cries:
rare, and I goe forward; at length I fling my Cap up; marke
there;
then do you, as once did Meleager and the Bore, break comly out
before him: like true lovers, cast your selves in a Body
decently,
and sweetly, by a figure trace and turne, Boyes.

1. COUNTREYMAN.

And sweetly we will doe it Master Gerrold.

2. COUNTREYMAN.

Draw up the Company. Where's the Taborour?

3. COUNTREYMAN.

Why, Timothy!

TABORER.

Here, my mad boyes, have at ye.

SCHOOLMASTER.

But I say, where's their women?

4. COUNTREYMAN.

Here's Friz and Maudline.

2. COUNTREYMAN.

And little Luce with the white legs, and bouncing Barbery.

1. COUNTREYMAN.

And freckeled Nel, that never faild her Master.

SCHOOLMASTER.

Wher be your Ribands, maids? swym with your Bodies
And carry it sweetly, and deliverly
And now and then a fauour, and a friske.

NEL.

Let us alone, Sir.

SCHOOLMASTER.

Wher's the rest o'th Musicke?

3. COUNTREYMAN.

Dispersd as you commanded.

SCHOOLMASTER.

Couple, then,
And see what's wanting; wher's the Bavian?
My friend, carry your taile without offence
Or scandall to the Ladies; and be sure
You tumble with audacity and manhood;
And when you barke, doe it with judgement.

BAVIAN.

Yes, Sir.

SCHOOLMASTER.

Quo usque tandem? Here is a woman wanting.

4. COUNTREYMAN.

We may goe whistle: all the fat's i'th fire.

SCHOOLMASTER.

We have,
As learned Authours utter, washd a Tile,
We have beene FATUUS, and laboured vainely.

2. COUNTREYMAN.

This is that scornefull peece, that scurvy hilding,
That gave her promise faithfully, she would be here,
Cicely the Sempsters daughter:
The next gloves that I give her shall be dog skin;
Nay and she faile me once—you can tell, Arcas,
She swore by wine and bread, she would not breake.

SCHOOLMASTER.

An Eele and woman,
A learned Poet sayes, unles by'th taile
And with thy teeth thou hold, will either faile.
In manners this was false position

1. COUNTREYMAN.

A fire ill take her; do's she flinch now?

3. COUNTREYMAN.

What
Shall we determine, Sir?

SCHOOLMASTER.

Nothing.
Our busines is become a nullity;
Yea, and a woefull, and a pittious nullity.

4. COUNTREYMAN.

Now when the credite of our Towne lay on it,
Now to be frampall, now to pisse o'th nettle!
Goe thy waies; ile remember thee, ile fit thee.

[Enter Iaylors daughter.]

DAUGHTER.

[Sings.]

The George alow came from the South,
From the coast of Barbary a.
And there he met with brave gallants of war
By one, by two, by three, a.

Well haild, well haild, you jolly gallants,
And whither now are you bound a?
O let me have your company *[Chaire and stooles out.]*
Till (I) come to the sound a.

There was three fooles, fell out about an howlet:
The one sed it was an owle,
The other he sed nay,
The third he sed it was a hawke,
And her bels wer cut away.

3. COUNTREYMAN.

Ther's a dainty mad woman M(aiste)r
Comes i'th Nick, as mad as a march hare:
If wee can get her daunce, wee are made againe:
I warrant her, shee'l doe the rarest gambols.

1. COUNTREYMAN.

A mad woman? we are made, Boyes.

SCHOOLMASTER.

And are you mad, good woman?

DAUGHTER.

I would be sorry else;
Give me your hand.

SCHOOLMASTER.

Why?

DAUGHTER.

I can tell your fortune.
You are a foole: tell ten. I have pozd him: Buz!
Friend you must eate no whitebread; if you doe,
Your teeth will bleede extreamely. Shall we dance, ho?
I know you, y'ar a Tinker: Sirha Tinker,
Stop no more holes, but what you should.

SCHOOLMASTER.

Dij boni. A Tinker, Damzell?

DAUGHTER.

Or a Conjurer:
Raise me a devill now, and let him play
Quipassa o'th bels and bones.

SCHOOLMASTER.

Goe, take her,
And fluently perswade her to a peace:
Et opus exegi, quod nec Iouis ira, nec ignis.
Strike up, and leade her in.

2. COUNTREYMAN.

Come, Lasse, lets trip it.

DAUGHTER.

Ile leade. *[Winde Hornes.]*

3. COUNTREYMAN.

Doe, doe.

SCHOOLMASTER.

Perswasively, and cunningly: away, boyes, *[Ex. all but
Schoolemaster.]*
I heare the hornes: give me some meditation,
And marke your Cue.—Pallas inspire me.

[Enter Thes. Pir. Hip. Emil. Arcite, and traine.]

THESEUS.

This way the Stag tooke.

SCHOOLMASTER.

Stay, and edifie.

THESEUS.

What have we here?

PERITHOUS.

Some Countrey sport, upon my life, Sir.

THESEUS.

Well, Sir, goe forward, we will edifie.
Ladies, sit downe, wee'l stay it.

SCHOOLMASTER.

Thou, doughtie Duke, all haile: all haile, sweet Ladies.

THESEUS.

This is a cold beginning.

SCHOOLMASTER.

If you but favour, our Country pastime made is.
We are a few of those collected here,
That ruder Tongues distinguish villager;
And to say veritie, and not to fable,
We are a merry rout, or else a rable,
Or company, or, by a figure, Choris,
That fore thy dignitie will dance a Morris.
And I, that am the rectifier of all,
By title Pedagogus, that let fall
The Birch upon the breeches of the small ones,
And humble with a Ferula the tall ones,
Doe here present this Machine, or this frame:
And daintie Duke, whose doughtie dismall fame
From Dis to Dedalus, from post to pillar,
Is blowne abroad, helpe me thy poore well willer,
And with thy twinckling eyes looke right and straight
Vpon this mighty MORR—of mickle waight;
IS now comes in, which being glewd together,
Makes MORRIS, and the cause that we came hether.

91

The body of our sport, of no small study,
I first appeare, though rude, and raw, and muddy,
To speake before thy noble grace this tenner:
At whose great feete I offer up my penner.
The next the Lord of May and Lady bright,
The Chambermaid and Servingman by night
That seeke out silent hanging: Then mine Host
And his fat Spowse, that welcomes to their cost
The gauled Traveller, and with a beckning
Informes the Tapster to inflame the reckning:
Then the beast eating Clowne, and next the foole,
The Bavian, with long tayle and eke long toole,
Cum multis alijs that make a dance:
Say 'I,' and all shall presently advance.

THESEUS.

I, I, by any meanes, deere Domine.

PERITHOUS.

Produce.

(SCHOOLMASTER.)

Intrate, filij; Come forth, and foot it.—

[Musicke, Dance. Knocke for Schoole.]

[Enter the Dance.]

Ladies, if we have beene merry,
And have pleasd yee with a derry,
And a derry, and a downe,
Say the Schoolemaster's no Clowne:
Duke, if we have pleasd thee too,

And have done as good Boyes should doe,
Give us but a tree or twaine
For a Maypole, and againe,
Ere another yeare run out,
Wee'l make thee laugh and all this rout.

THESEUS.

Take 20., Domine; how does my sweet heart?

HIPPOLITA.

Never so pleasd, Sir.

EMILIA.

Twas an excellent dance, and for a preface
I never heard a better.

THESEUS.

Schoolemaster, I thanke you.—One see'em all rewarded.

PERITHOUS.

And heer's something to paint your Pole withall.

THESEUS.

Now to our sports againe.

SCHOOLMASTER.

May the Stag thou huntst stand long,
And thy dogs be swift and strong:
May they kill him without lets,

And the Ladies eate his dowsets!
Come, we are all made. *[Winde Hornes.]*
Dij Deoeq(ue) omnes, ye have danc'd rarely, wenches. *[Exeunt.]*

Scaena 6. (Same as Scene III.)

[Enter Palamon from the Bush.]

PALAMON.

About this houre my Cosen gave his faith
To visit me againe, and with him bring
Two Swords, and two good Armors; if he faile,
He's neither man nor Souldier. When he left me,
I did not thinke a weeke could have restord
My lost strength to me, I was growne so low,
And Crest–falne with my wants: I thanke thee, Arcite,
Thou art yet a faire Foe; and I feele my selfe
With this refreshing, able once againe
To out dure danger: To delay it longer
Would make the world think, when it comes to hearing,
That I lay fatting like a Swine to fight,
And not a Souldier: Therefore, this blest morning
Shall be the last; and that Sword he refuses,
If it but hold, I kill him with; tis Iustice:
So love, and Fortune for me!—O, good morrow.

[Enter Arcite with Armors and Swords.]

ARCITE.

Good morrow, noble kinesman.

PALAMON.

I have put you to too much paines, Sir.

ARCITE.

That too much, faire Cosen,
Is but a debt to honour, and my duty.

PALAMON.

Would you were so in all, Sir; I could wish ye
As kinde a kinsman, as you force me finde
A beneficiall foe, that my embraces
Might thanke ye, not my blowes.

ARCITE.

I shall thinke either, well done,
A noble recompence.

PALAMON.

Then I shall quit you.

ARCITE.

Defy me in these faire termes, and you show
More then a Mistris to me, no more anger
As you love any thing that's honourable:
We were not bred to talke, man; when we are arm'd
And both upon our guards, then let our fury,

Like meeting of two tides, fly strongly from us,
And then to whom the birthright of this Beauty
Truely pertaines (without obbraidings, scornes,
Dispisings of our persons, and such powtings,
Fitter for Girles and Schooleboyes) will be seene
And quickly, yours, or mine: wilt please you arme, Sir,
Or if you feele your selfe not fitting yet
And furnishd with your old strength, ile stay, Cosen,
And ev'ry day discourse you into health,
As I am spard: your person I am friends with,
And I could wish I had not saide I lov'd her,
Though I had dide; But loving such a Lady
And justifying my Love, I must not fly from't.

PALAMON.

Arcite, thou art so brave an enemy,
That no man but thy Cosen's fit to kill thee:
I am well and lusty, choose your Armes.

ARCITE.

Choose you, Sir.

PALAMON.

Wilt thou exceede in all, or do'st thou doe it
To make me spare thee?

ARCITE.

If you thinke so, Cosen,
You are deceived, for as I am a Soldier,
I will not spare you.

PALAMON.

That's well said.

ARCITE.

You'l finde it.

PALAMON.

Then, as I am an honest man and love
With all the justice of affection,
Ile pay thee soundly. This ile take.

ARCITE.

That's mine, then;
Ile arme you first.

PALAMON.

Do: pray thee, tell me, Cosen,
Where gotst thou this good Armour?

ARCITE.

Tis the Dukes,
And to say true, I stole it; doe I pinch you?

PALAMON.

Noe.

ARCITE.

Is't not too heavie?

PALAMON.

I have worne a lighter,
But I shall make it serve.

ARCITE.

Ile buckl't close.

PALAMON.

By any meanes.

ARCITE.

You care not for a Grand guard?

PALAMON.

No, no; wee'l use no horses: I perceave
You would faine be at that Fight.

ARCITE.

I am indifferent.

PALAMON.

Faith, so am I: good Cosen, thrust the buckle
Through far enough.

ARCITE.

I warrant you.

PALAMON.

My Caske now.

ARCITE.

Will you fight bare−armd?

PALAMON.

We shall be the nimbler.

ARCITE.

But use your Gauntlets though; those are o'th least,
Prethee take mine, good Cosen.

PALAMON.

Thanke you, Arcite.
How doe I looke? am I falne much away?

ARCITE.

Faith, very little; love has usd you kindly.

PALAMON.

Ile warrant thee, Ile strike home.

ARCITE.

Doe, and spare not;
Ile give you cause, sweet Cosen.

PALAMON.

Now to you, Sir:
Me thinkes this Armor's very like that, Arcite,
Thou wor'st the day the 3. Kings fell, but lighter.

ARCITE.

That was a very good one; and that day,
I well remember, you outdid me, Cosen.
I never saw such valour: when you chargd
Vpon the left wing of the Enemie,
I spurd hard to come up, and under me
I had a right good horse.

PALAMON.

You had indeede; a bright Bay, I remember.

ARCITE.

Yes, but all
Was vainely labour'd in me; you outwent me,
Nor could my wishes reach you; yet a little
I did by imitation.

PALAMON.

More by vertue;
You are modest, Cosen.

ARCITE.

When I saw you charge first,
Me thought I heard a dreadfull clap of Thunder
Breake from the Troope.

PALAMON.

But still before that flew
The lightning of your valour. Stay a little,
Is not this peece too streight?

ARCITE.

No, no, tis well.

PALAMON.

I would have nothing hurt thee but my Sword,
A bruise would be dishonour.

ARCITE.

Now I am perfect.

PALAMON.

Stand off, then.

ARCITE.

Take my Sword, I hold it better.

PALAMON.

I thanke ye: No, keepe it; your life lyes on it.
Here's one; if it but hold, I aske no more
For all my hopes: My Cause and honour guard me! *[They bow
severall wayes: then advance and stand.]*

ARCITE.

And me my love! Is there ought else to say?

PALAMON.

This onely, and no more: Thou art mine Aunts Son,
And that blood we desire to shed is mutuall;
In me, thine, and in thee, mine. My Sword
Is in my hand, and if thou killst me,
The gods and I forgive thee; If there be
A place prepar'd for those that sleepe in honour,
I wish his wearie soule that falls may win it:
Fight bravely, Cosen; give me thy noble hand.

ARCITE.

Here, Palamon: This hand shall never more
Come neare thee with such friendship.

PALAMON.

I commend thee.

ARCITE.

If I fall, curse me, and say I was a coward,
For none but such dare die in these just Tryalls.
Once more farewell, my Cosen.

PALAMON.

Farewell, Arcite. *[Fight.]*

[Hornes within: they stand.]

ARCITE.

Loe, Cosen, loe, our Folly has undon us.

PALAMON.

Why?

ARCITE.

This is the Duke, a hunting as I told you.
If we be found, we are wretched. O retire
For honours sake, and safety presently
Into your Bush agen; Sir, we shall finde
Too many howres to dye in: gentle Cosen,
If you be seene you perish instantly
For breaking prison, and I, if you reveale me,
For my contempt. Then all the world will scorne us,
And say we had a noble difference,
But base disposers of it.

PALAMON.

No, no, Cosen,
I will no more be hidden, nor put off
This great adventure to a second Tryall:
I know your cunning, and I know your cause;
He that faints now, shame take him: put thy selfe
Vpon thy present guard—

ARCITE.

You are not mad?

PALAMON.

Or I will make th'advantage of this howre
Mine owne, and what to come shall threaten me,
I feare lesse then my fortune: know, weake Cosen,

I love Emilia, and in that ile bury
Thee, and all crosses else.

ARCITE.

Then, come what can come,
Thou shalt know, Palamon, I dare as well
Die, as discourse, or sleepe: Onely this feares me,
The law will have the honour of our ends.
Have at thy life.

PALAMON.

Looke to thine owne well, Arcite. *[Fight againe. Hornes.]*

[Enter Theseus, Hipolita, Emilia, Perithous and traine.]

THESEUS.

What ignorant and mad malicious Traitors,
Are you, That gainst the tenor of my Lawes
Are making Battaile, thus like Knights appointed,
Without my leave, and Officers of Armes?
By Castor, both shall dye.

PALAMON.

Hold thy word, Theseus.
We are certainly both Traitors, both despisers
Of thee and of thy goodnesse: I am Palamon,
That cannot love thee, he that broke thy Prison;
Thinke well what that deserves: and this is Arcite,
A bolder Traytor never trod thy ground,
A Falser neu'r seem'd friend: This is the man
Was begd and banish'd; this is he contemnes thee
And what thou dar'st doe, and in this disguise

Against thy owne Edict followes thy Sister,
That fortunate bright Star, the faire Emilia,
Whose servant, (if there be a right in seeing,
And first bequeathing of the soule to) justly
I am, and, which is more, dares thinke her his.
This treacherie, like a most trusty Lover,
I call'd him now to answer; if thou bee'st,
As thou art spoken, great and vertuous,
The true descider of all injuries,
Say, 'Fight againe,' and thou shalt see me, Theseus,
Doe such a Iustice, thou thy selfe wilt envie.
Then take my life; Ile wooe thee too't.

PERITHOUS.

O heaven,
What more then man is this!

THESEUS.

I have sworne.

ARCITE.

We seeke not
Thy breath of mercy, Theseus. Tis to me
A thing as soone to dye, as thee to say it,
And no more mov'd: where this man calls me Traitor,
Let me say thus much: if in love be Treason,
In service of so excellent a Beutie,
As I love most, and in that faith will perish,
As I have brought my life here to confirme it,
As I have serv'd her truest, worthiest,
As I dare kill this Cosen, that denies it,
So let me be most Traitor, and ye please me.
For scorning thy Edict, Duke, aske that Lady

Why she is faire, and why her eyes command me
Stay here to love her; and if she say 'Traytor,'
I am a villaine fit to lye unburied.

PALAMON.

Thou shalt have pitty of us both, o Theseus,
If unto neither thou shew mercy; stop
(As thou art just) thy noble eare against us.
As thou art valiant, for thy Cosens soule
Whose 12. strong labours crowne his memory,
Lets die together, at one instant, Duke,
Onely a little let him fall before me,
That I may tell my Soule he shall not have her.

THESEUS.

I grant your wish, for, to say true, your Cosen
Has ten times more offended; for I gave him
More mercy then you found, Sir, your offenses
Being no more then his. None here speake for 'em,
For, ere the Sun set, both shall sleepe for ever.

HIPPOLITA.

Alas the pitty! now or never, Sister,
Speake, not to be denide; That face of yours
Will beare the curses else of after ages
For these lost Cosens.

EMILIA.

In my face, deare Sister,
I finde no anger to 'em, nor no ruyn;
The misadventure of their owne eyes kill 'em;
Yet that I will be woman, and have pitty,

My knees shall grow to'th ground but Ile get mercie.
Helpe me, deare Sister; in a deede so vertuous
The powers of all women will be with us.
Most royall Brother—

HIPPOLITA.

Sir, by our tye of Marriage—

EMILIA.

By your owne spotlesse honour—

HIPPOLITA.

By that faith,
That faire hand, and that honest heart you gave me.

EMILIA.

By that you would have pitty in another,
By your owne vertues infinite.

HIPPOLITA.

By valour,
By all the chaste nights I have ever pleasd you.

THESEUS.

These are strange Conjurings.

PERITHOUS.

Nay, then, Ile in too:
By all our friendship, Sir, by all our dangers,

By all you love most: warres and this sweet Lady.

EMILIA.

By that you would have trembled to deny,
A blushing Maide.

HIPPOLITA.

By your owne eyes: By strength,
In which you swore I went beyond all women,
Almost all men, and yet I yeelded, Theseus.

PERITHOUS.

To crowne all this: By your most noble soule,
Which cannot want due mercie, I beg first.

HIPPOLITA.

Next, heare my prayers.

EMILIA.

Last, let me intreate, Sir.

PERITHOUS.

For mercy.

HIPPOLITA.

Mercy.

EMILIA.

Mercy on these Princes.

THESEUS.

Ye make my faith reele: Say I felt
Compassion to'em both, how would you place it?

EMILIA.

Vpon their lives: But with their banishments.

THESEUS.

You are a right woman, Sister; you have pitty,
But want the vnderstanding where to use it.
If you desire their lives, invent a way
Safer then banishment: Can these two live
And have the agony of love about 'em,
And not kill one another? Every day
They'ld fight about you; howrely bring your honour
In publique question with their Swords. Be wise, then,
And here forget 'em; it concernes your credit
And my oth equally: I have said they die;
Better they fall by'th law, then one another.
Bow not my honor.

EMILIA.

O my noble Brother,
That oth was rashly made, and in your anger,
Your reason will not hold it; if such vowes
Stand for expresse will, all the world must perish.
Beside, I have another oth gainst yours,
Of more authority, I am sure more love,
Not made in passion neither, but good heede.

THESEUS.

What is it, Sister?

PERITHOUS.

Vrge it home, brave Lady.

EMILIA.

That you would nev'r deny me any thing
Fit for my modest suit, and your free granting:
I tye you to your word now; if ye fall in't,
Thinke how you maime your honour,
(For now I am set a begging, Sir, I am deafe
To all but your compassion.) How, their lives
Might breed the ruine of my name, Opinion!
Shall any thing that loves me perish for me?
That were a cruell wisedome; doe men proyne
The straight yong Bowes that blush with thousand Blossoms,
Because they may be rotten? O Duke Theseus,
The goodly Mothers that have groand for these,
And all the longing Maides that ever lov'd,
If your vow stand, shall curse me and my Beauty,
And in their funerall songs for these two Cosens
Despise my crueltie, and cry woe worth me,
Till I am nothing but the scorne of women;
For heavens sake save their lives, and banish 'em.

THESEUS.

On what conditions?

EMILIA.

Sweare'em never more

To make me their Contention, or to know me,
To tread upon thy Dukedome; and to be,
Where ever they shall travel, ever strangers
To one another.

PALAMON.

Ile be cut a peeces
Before I take this oth: forget I love her?
O all ye gods dispise me, then! Thy Banishment
I not mislike, so we may fairely carry
Our Swords and cause along: else, never trifle,
But take our lives, Duke: I must love and will,
And for that love must and dare kill this Cosen
On any peece the earth has.

THESEUS.

Will you, Arcite,
Take these conditions?

PALAMON.

He's a villaine, then.

PERITHOUS.

These are men.

ARCITE.

No, never, Duke: Tis worse to me than begging
To take my life so basely; though I thinke
I never shall enjoy her, yet ile preserve
The honour of affection, and dye for her,
Make death a Devill.

THESEUS.

What may be done? for now I feele compassion.

PERITHOUS.

Let it not fall agen, Sir.

THESEUS.

Say, Emilia,
If one of them were dead, as one must, are you
Content to take th'other to your husband?
They cannot both enjoy you; They are Princes
As goodly as your owne eyes, and as noble
As ever fame yet spoke of; looke upon 'em,
And if you can love, end this difference.
I give consent; are you content too, Princes?

BOTH.

With all our soules.

THESEUS.

He that she refuses
Must dye, then.

BOTH.

Any death thou canst invent, Duke.

PALAMON.

If I fall from that mouth, I fall with favour,

112

And Lovers yet unborne shall blesse my ashes.

ARCITE.

If she refuse me, yet my grave will wed me,
And Souldiers sing my Epitaph.

THESEUS.

Make choice, then.

EMILIA.

I cannot, Sir, they are both too excellent:
For me, a hayre shall never fall of these men.

HIPPOLITA.

What will become of 'em?

THESEUS.

Thus I ordaine it;
And by mine honor, once againe, it stands,
Or both shall dye:—You shall both to your Countrey,
And each within this moneth, accompanied
With three faire Knights, appeare againe in this place,
In which Ile plant a Pyramid; and whether,
Before us that are here, can force his Cosen
By fayre and knightly strength to touch the Pillar,
He shall enjoy her: the other loose his head,
And all his friends; Nor shall he grudge to fall,
Nor thinke he dies with interest in this Lady:
Will this content yee?

PALAMON.

Yes: here, Cosen Arcite,
I am friends againe, till that howre.

ARCITE.

I embrace ye.

THESEUS.

Are you content, Sister?

EMILIA.

Yes, I must, Sir,
Els both miscarry.

THESEUS.

Come, shake hands againe, then;
And take heede, as you are Gentlemen, this Quarrell
Sleepe till the howre prefixt; and hold your course.

PALAMON.

We dare not faile thee, Theseus.

THESEUS.

Come, Ile give ye
Now usage like to Princes, and to Friends:
When ye returne, who wins, Ile settle heere;
Who looses, yet Ile weepe upon his Beere. *[Exeunt.]*

Actus Quartus.

Scaena 1. (Athens. A room in the prison.)

[Enter Iailor and his friend.]

IAILOR.

Heare you no more? was nothing saide of me
Concerning the escape of Palamon?
Good Sir, remember.

1. FRIEND.

Nothing that I heard,
For I came home before the busines
Was fully ended: Yet I might perceive,
Ere I departed, a great likelihood
Of both their pardons: For Hipolita,
And faire–eyd Emilie, upon their knees
Begd with such hansom pitty, that the Duke
Me thought stood staggering, whether he should follow
His rash oth, or the sweet compassion
Of those two Ladies; and to second them,
That truely noble Prince Perithous,

Halfe his owne heart, set in too, that I hope
All shall be well: Neither heard I one question
Of your name or his scape.

[Enter 2. Friend.]

IAILOR.

Pray heaven it hold so.

2. FRIEND.

Be of good comfort, man; I bring you newes,
Good newes.

IAILOR.

They are welcome,

2. FRIEND.

Palamon has cleerd you,
And got your pardon, and discoverd how
And by whose meanes he escapt, which was your Daughters,
Whose pardon is procurd too; and the Prisoner,
Not to be held ungratefull to her goodnes,
Has given a summe of money to her Marriage,
A large one, ile assure you.

IAILOR.

Ye are a good man
And ever bring good newes.

1. FRIEND.

How was it ended?

2. FRIEND.

Why, as it should be; they that nev'r begd
But they prevaild, had their suites fairely granted,
The prisoners have their lives.

1. FRIEND.

I knew t'would be so.

2. FRIEND.

But there be new conditions, which you'l heare of
At better time.

IAILOR.

I hope they are good.

2. FRIEND.

They are honourable,
How good they'l prove, I know not.

[Enter Wooer.]

1. FRIEND.

T'will be knowne.

WOOER.

Alas, Sir, wher's your Daughter?

IAILOR.

Why doe you aske?

WOOER.

O, Sir, when did you see her?

2. FRIEND.

How he lookes?

IAILOR.

This morning.

WOOER.

Was she well? was she in health, Sir?
When did she sleepe?

1. FRIEND.

These are strange Questions.

IAILOR.

I doe not thinke she was very well, for now
You make me minde her, but this very day
I ask'd her questions, and she answered me
So farre from what she was, so childishly,
So sillily, as if she were a foole,
An Inocent, and I was very angry.
But what of her, Sir?

WOOER.

Nothing but my pitty;
But you must know it, and as good by me
As by an other that lesse loves her—

IAILOR.

Well, Sir.

1. FRIEND.

Not right?

2. FRIEND.

Not well?

WOOER.

No, Sir, not well.
Tis too true, she is mad.

1. FRIEND.

It cannot be.

WOOER.

Beleeve, you'l finde it so.

IAILOR.

I halfe suspected
What you (have) told me: the gods comfort her:
Either this was her love to Palamon,
Or feare of my miscarrying on his scape,

Or both.

WOOER.

Tis likely.

IAILOR.

But why all this haste, Sir?

WOOER.

Ile tell you quickly. As I late was angling
In the great Lake that lies behind the Pallace,
From the far shore, thicke set with reedes and Sedges,
As patiently I was attending sport,
I heard a voyce, a shrill one, and attentive
I gave my eare, when I might well perceive
T'was one that sung, and by the smallnesse of it
A boy or woman. I then left my angle
To his owne skill, came neere, but yet perceivd not
Who made the sound, the rushes and the Reeds
Had so encompast it: I laide me downe
And listned to the words she sung, for then,
Through a small glade cut by the Fisher men,
I saw it was your Daughter.

IAILOR.

Pray, goe on, Sir?

WOOER.

She sung much, but no sence; onely I heard her
Repeat this often: 'Palamon is gone,
Is gone to'th wood to gather Mulberies;

Ile finde him out to morrow.'

1. FRIEND.

Pretty soule.

WOOER.

'His shackles will betray him, hee'l be taken,
And what shall I doe then? Ile bring a beavy,
A hundred blacke eyd Maides, that love as I doe,
With Chaplets on their heads of Daffadillies,
With cherry–lips, and cheekes of Damaske Roses,
And all wee'l daunce an Antique fore the Duke,
And beg his pardon.' Then she talk'd of you, Sir;
That you must loose your head to morrow morning,
And she must gather flowers to bury you,
And see the house made handsome: then she sung
Nothing but 'Willow, willow, willow,' and betweene
Ever was, 'Palamon, faire Palamon,'
And 'Palamon was a tall yong man.' The place
Was knee deepe where she sat; her careles Tresses
A wreathe of bull–rush rounded; about her stucke
Thousand fresh water flowers of severall cullors,
That me thought she appeard like the faire Nimph
That feedes the lake with waters, or as Iris
Newly dropt downe from heaven; Rings she made
Of rushes that grew by, and to 'em spoke
The prettiest posies: 'Thus our true love's tide,'
'This you may loose, not me,' and many a one:
And then she wept, and sung againe, and sigh'd,
And with the same breath smil'd, and kist her hand.

2. FRIEND.

Alas, what pitty it is!

WOOER.

I made in to her.
She saw me, and straight sought the flood; I sav'd her,
And set her safe to land: when presently
She slipt away, and to the Citty made,
With such a cry and swiftnes, that, beleeve me,
Shee left me farre behinde her; three or foure
I saw from farre off crosse her, one of 'em
I knew to be your brother; where she staid,
And fell, scarce to be got away: I left them with her, *[Enter
Brother, Daughter, and others.]*
And hether came to tell you. Here they are.

DAUGHTER. *[sings.]*

May you never more enjoy the light, c.

Is not this a fine Song?

BROTHER.

O, a very fine one.

DAUGHTER.

I can sing twenty more.

BROTHER.

I thinke you can.

DAUGHTER.

Yes, truely, can I; I can sing the Broome,

And Bony Robin. Are not you a tailour?

BROTHER.

Yes.

DAUGHTER.

Wher's my wedding Gowne?

BROTHER.

Ile bring it to morrow.

DAUGHTER.

Doe, very rarely; I must be abroad else
To call the Maides, and pay the Minstrels,
For I must loose my Maydenhead by cock—light;
Twill never thrive else.
[Singes.] O faire, oh sweete, c.

BROTHER.

You must ev'n take it patiently.

IAILOR.

Tis true.

DAUGHTER.

Good ev'n, good men; pray, did you ever heare
Of one yong Palamon?

IAILOR.

Yes, wench, we know him.

DAUGHTER.

Is't not a fine yong Gentleman?

IAILOR.

Tis Love.

BROTHER.

By no meane crosse her; she is then distemperd
Far worse then now she showes.

1. FRIEND.

Yes, he's a fine man.

DAUGHTER.

O, is he so? you have a Sister?

1. FRIEND.

Yes.

DAUGHTER.

But she shall never have him, tell her so,
For a tricke that I know; y'had best looke to her,
For if she see him once, she's gone, she's done,
And undon in an howre. All the young Maydes
Of our Towne are in love with him, but I laugh at 'em
And let 'em all alone; Is't not a wise course?

1. FRIEND.

Yes.

DAUGHTER.

There is at least two hundred now with child by him—
There must be fowre; yet I keepe close for all this,
Close as a Cockle; and all these must be Boyes,
He has the tricke on't, and at ten yeares old
They must be all gelt for Musitians,
And sing the wars of Theseus.

2. FRIEND.

This is strange.

DAUGHTER.

As ever you heard, but say nothing.

1. FRIEND.

No.

DAUGHTER.

They come from all parts of the Dukedome to him;
Ile warrant ye, he had not so few last night
As twenty to dispatch: hee'l tickl't up
In two howres, if his hand be in.

IAILOR.

She's lost

Past all cure.

BROTHER.

Heaven forbid, man.

DAUGHTER.

Come hither, you are a wise man.

1. FRIEND.

Do's she know him?

2. FRIEND.

No, would she did.

DAUGHTER.

You are master of a Ship?

IAILOR.

Yes.

DAUGHTER.

Wher's your Compasse?

IAILOR.

Heere.

DAUGHTER.

Set it too'th North.
And now direct your course to'th wood, wher Palamon
Lyes longing for me; For the Tackling
Let me alone; Come, waygh, my hearts, cheerely!

ALL.

Owgh, owgh, owgh, tis up, the wind's faire,
Top the Bowling, out with the maine saile;
Wher's your Whistle, Master?

BROTHER.

Lets get her in.

IAILOR.

Vp to the top, Boy.

BROTHER.

Wher's the Pilot?

1. FRIEND.

Heere.

DAUGHTER.

What ken'st thou?

2. FRIEND.

A faire wood.

DAUGHTER.

Beare for it, master: take about! *[Singes.]*
When Cinthia with her borrowed light, c. *[Exeunt.]*

Scaena 2. (A Room in the Palace.)

[Enter Emilia alone, with 2. Pictures.]

EMILIA.

Yet I may binde those wounds up, that must open
And bleed to death for my sake else; Ile choose,
And end their strife: Two such yong hansom men
Shall never fall for me, their weeping Mothers,
Following the dead cold ashes of their Sonnes,
Shall never curse my cruelty. Good heaven,
What a sweet face has Arcite! if wise nature,
With all her best endowments, all those beuties
She sowes into the birthes of noble bodies,
Were here a mortall woman, and had in her
The coy denialls of yong Maydes, yet doubtles,
She would run mad for this man: what an eye,
Of what a fyry sparkle, and quick sweetnes,
Has this yong Prince! Here Love himselfe sits smyling,
Iust such another wanton Ganimead
Set Jove a fire with, and enforcd the god
Snatch up the goodly Boy, and set him by him
A shining constellation: What a brow,
Of what a spacious Majesty, he carries!

Arch'd like the great eyd Iuno's, but far sweeter,
Smoother then Pelops Shoulder! Fame and honour,
Me thinks, from hence, as from a Promontory
Pointed in heaven, should clap their wings, and sing
To all the under world the Loves and Fights
Of gods, and such men neere 'em. Palamon
Is but his foyle, to him a meere dull shadow:
Hee's swarth and meagre, of an eye as heavy
As if he had lost his mother; a still temper,
No stirring in him, no alacrity,
Of all this sprightly sharpenes not a smile;
Yet these that we count errours may become him:
Narcissus was a sad Boy, but a heavenly:—
Oh who can finde the bent of womans fancy?
I am a Foole, my reason is lost in me;
I have no choice, and I have ly'd so lewdly
That women ought to beate me. On my knees
I aske thy pardon, Palamon; thou art alone,
And only beutifull, and these the eyes,
These the bright lamps of beauty, that command
And threaten Love, and what yong Mayd dare crosse 'em?
What a bold gravity, and yet inviting,
Has this browne manly face! O Love, this only
From this howre is Complexion: Lye there, Arcite,
Thou art a changling to him, a meere Gipsey,
And this the noble Bodie. I am sotted,
Vtterly lost: My Virgins faith has fled me;
For if my brother but even now had ask'd me
Whether I lov'd, I had run mad for Arcite;
Now, if my Sister, More for Palamon.
Stand both together: Now, come aske me, Brother.—
Alas, I know not! Aske me now, sweet Sister;—
I may goe looke. What a meere child is Fancie,
That, having two faire gawdes of equall sweetnesse,
Cannot distinguish, but must crie for both.

[Enter (a) Gent(leman.)]

EMILIA.

How now, Sir?

GENTLEMAN.

From the Noble Duke your Brother,
Madam, I bring you newes: The Knights are come.

EMILIA.

To end the quarrell?

GENTLEMAN.

Yes.

EMILIA.

Would I might end first:
What sinnes have I committed, chast Diana,
That my unspotted youth must now be soyld
With blood of Princes? and my Chastitie
Be made the Altar, where the lives of Lovers
(Two greater and two better never yet
Made mothers joy) must be the sacrifice
To my unhappy Beautie?

[Enter Theseus, Hipolita, Perithous and attendants.]

THESEUS.

Bring 'em in
Quickly, By any meanes; I long to see 'em.—

Your two contending Lovers are return'd,
And with them their faire Knights: Now, my faire Sister,
You must love one of them.

EMILIA.

I had rather both,
So neither for my sake should fall untimely.

[Enter Messenger. (Curtis.)]

THESEUS.

Who saw 'em?

PERITHOUS.

I, a while.

GENTLEMAN.

And I.

THESEUS.

From whence come you, Sir?

MESSENGER.

From the Knights.

THESEUS.

Pray, speake,
You that have seene them, what they are.

MESSENGER.

I will, Sir,
And truly what I thinke: Six braver spirits
Then these they have brought, (if we judge by the outside)
I never saw, nor read of. He that stands
In the first place with Arcite, by his seeming,
Should be a stout man, by his face a Prince,
(His very lookes so say him) his complexion,
Nearer a browne, than blacke, sterne, and yet noble,
Which shewes him hardy, fearelesse, proud of dangers:
The circles of his eyes show fire within him,
And as a heated Lyon, so he lookes;
His haire hangs long behind him, blacke and shining
Like Ravens wings: his shoulders broad and strong,
Armd long and round, and on his Thigh a Sword
Hung by a curious Bauldricke, when he frownes
To seale his will with: better, o'my conscience
Was never Souldiers friend.

THESEUS.

Thou ha'st well describde him.

PERITHOUS.

Yet a great deale short,
Me thinkes, of him that's first with Palamon.

THESEUS.

Pray, speake him, friend.

PERITHOUS.

I ghesse he is a Prince too,

And, if it may be, greater; for his show
Has all the ornament of honour in't:
Hee's somewhat bigger, then the Knight he spoke of,
But of a face far sweeter; His complexion
Is (as a ripe grape) ruddy: he has felt,
Without doubt, what he fights for, and so apter
To make this cause his owne: In's face appeares
All the faire hopes of what he undertakes,
And when he's angry, then a setled valour
(Not tainted with extreames) runs through his body,
And guides his arme to brave things: Feare he cannot,
He shewes no such soft temper; his head's yellow,
Hard hayr'd, and curld, thicke twind like Ivy tods,
Not to undoe with thunder; In his face
The liverie of the warlike Maide appeares,
Pure red, and white, for yet no beard has blest him.
And in his rowling eyes sits victory,
As if she ever ment to court his valour:
His Nose stands high, a Character of honour.
His red lips, after fights, are fit for Ladies.

EMILIA.

Must these men die too?

PERITHOUS.

When he speakes, his tongue
Sounds like a Trumpet; All his lyneaments
Are as a man would wish 'em, strong and cleane,
He weares a well–steeld Axe, the staffe of gold;
His age some five and twenty.

MESSENGER.

Ther's another,

A little man, but of a tough soule, seeming
As great as any: fairer promises
In such a Body yet I never look'd on.

PERITHOUS.

O, he that's freckle fac'd?

MESSENGER.

The same, my Lord;
Are they not sweet ones?

PERITHOUS.

Yes, they are well.

MESSENGER.

Me thinkes,
Being so few, and well disposd, they show
Great, and fine art in nature: he's white hair'd,
Not wanton white, but such a manly colour
Next to an aborne; tough, and nimble set,
Which showes an active soule; his armes are brawny,
Linde with strong sinewes: To the shoulder peece
Gently they swell, like women new conceav'd,
Which speakes him prone to labour, never fainting
Vnder the waight of Armes; stout harted, still,
But when he stirs, a Tiger; he's gray eyd,
Which yeelds compassion where he conquers: sharpe
To spy advantages, and where he finds 'em,
He's swift to make 'em his: He do's no wrongs,
Nor takes none; he's round fac'd, and when he smiles
He showes a Lover, when he frownes, a Souldier:
About his head he weares the winners oke,

And in it stucke the favour of his Lady:
His age, some six and thirtie. In his hand
He beares a charging Staffe, embost with silver.

THESEUS.

Are they all thus?

PERITHOUS.

They are all the sonnes of honour.

THESEUS.

Now, as I have a soule, I long to see'em.
Lady, you shall see men fight now.

HIPPOLITA.

I wish it,
But not the cause, my Lord; They would show
Bravely about the Titles of two Kingdomes;
Tis pitty Love should be so tyrannous:
O my soft harted Sister, what thinke you?
Weepe not, till they weepe blood, Wench; it must be.

THESEUS.

You have steel'd 'em with your Beautie.—Honord Friend,
To you I give the Feild; pray, order it
Fitting the persons that must use it.

PERITHOUS.

Yes, Sir.

THESEUS.

Come, Ile goe visit 'em: I cannot stay,
Their fame has fir'd me so; Till they appeare.
Good Friend, be royall.

PERITHOUS.

There shall want no bravery.

EMILIA.

Poore wench, goe weepe, for whosoever wins,
Looses a noble Cosen for thy sins. *[Exeunt.]*

Scaena 3. (A room in the prison.)

[Enter Iailor, Wooer, Doctor.]

DOCTOR.

Her distraction is more at some time of the Moone, then at other
some, is it not?

IAILOR.

She is continually in a harmelesse distemper, sleepes little,
altogether without appetite, save often drinking, dreaming of
another world, and a better; and what broken peece of matter

so'ere she's about, the name Palamon lardes it, that she farces
ev'ry busines withall, fyts it to every question.—

[Enter Daughter.]

Looke where shee comes, you shall perceive her behaviour.

DAUGHTER.

I have forgot it quite; The burden on't, was DOWNE A, DOWNE A,
and pend by no worse man, then Giraldo, Emilias Schoolemaster;
he's as Fantasticall too, as ever he may goe upon's legs,—for
in the next world will Dido see Palamon, and then will she be
out of love with Eneas.

DOCTOR.

What stuff's here? pore soule!

IAILOR.

Ev'n thus all day long.

DAUGHTER.

Now for this Charme, that I told you of: you must bring a peece
of silver on the tip of your tongue, or no ferry: then, if it be
your chance to come where the blessed spirits, as ther's a sight
now—we maids that have our Lyvers perish'd, crakt to peeces with
Love, we shall come there, and doe nothing all day long but picke
flowers with Proserpine; then will I make Palamon a Nosegay; then
let him marke me,—then—

DOCTOR.

How prettily she's amisse? note her a little further.

DAUGHTER.

Faith, ile tell you, sometime we goe to Barly breake, we of the
blessed; alas, tis a sore life they have i'th other place, such
burning, frying, boyling, hissing, howling, chattring, cursing,
oh they have shrowd measure! take heede; if one be mad, or hang
or drowne themselves, thither they goe, Iupiter blesse vs, and
there shall we be put in a Caldron of lead, and Vsurers grease,
amongst a whole million of cutpurses, and there boyle like a
Gamon
of Bacon that will never be enough. *[Exit.]*

DOCTOR.

How her braine coynes!

DAUGHTER.

Lords and Courtiers, that have got maids with Child, they are in
this place: they shall stand in fire up to the Nav'le, and in yce
up to'th hart, and there th'offending part burnes, and the
deceaving part freezes; in troth, a very greevous punishment, as
one would thinke, for such a Trifle; beleve me, one would marry a
leaprous witch, to be rid on't, Ile assure you.

DOCTOR.

How she continues this fancie! Tis not an engraffed Madnesse,
but a most thicke, and profound mellencholly.

DAUGHTER.

To heare there a proud Lady, and a proud Citty wiffe, howle
together! I were a beast and il'd call it good sport: one cries,
'O this smoake!' another, 'this fire!' One cries, 'O, that ever

I did it behind the arras!' and then howles; th'other curses a suing fellow and her garden house. *[Sings]* I will be true, my stars, my fate, c. *[Exit Daugh.]*

IAILOR.

What thinke you of her, Sir?

DOCTOR.

I thinke she has a perturbed minde, which I cannot minister to.

IAILOR.

Alas, what then?

DOCTOR.

Vnderstand you, she ever affected any man, ere she beheld Palamon?

IAILOR.

I was once, Sir, in great hope she had fixd her liking on this gentleman, my friend.

WOOER.

I did thinke so too, and would account I had a great pen–worth on't, to give halfe my state, that both she and I at this present stood unfainedly on the same tearmes.

DOCTOR.

That intemprat surfeit of her eye hath distemperd the other sences: they may returne and settle againe to execute their preordaind

faculties, but they are now in a most extravagant vagary. This
you must doe: Confine her to a place, where the light may rather
seeme to steale in, then be permitted; take vpon you (yong Sir,
her friend) the name of Palamon; say you come to eate with her,
and to commune of Love; this will catch her attention, for this
her minde beates upon; other objects that are inserted tweene her
minde and eye become the prankes and friskins of her madnes; Sing
to her such greene songs of Love, as she sayes Palamon hath sung
in prison; Come to her, stucke in as sweet flowers as the season
is mistres of, and thereto make an addition of som other compounded
odours, which are grateful to the sence: all this shall become
Palamon, for Palamon can sing, and Palamon is sweet, and ev'ry
good thing: desire to eate with her, carve her, drinke to her,
and still among, intermingle your petition of grace and acceptance
into her favour: Learne what Maides have beene her companions and
play–pheeres, and let them repaire to her with Palamon in their
mouthes, and appeare with tokens, as if they suggested for him.
It is a falsehood she is in, which is with falsehood to be combated.
This may bring her to eate, to sleepe, and reduce what's now out
of square in her, into their former law, and regiment; I have seene
it approved, how many times I know not, but to make the number more,
I have great hope in this. I will, betweene the passages of this
project, come in with my applyance: Let us put it in execution,
and hasten the successe, which, doubt not, will bring forth
comfort. *[Florish. Exeunt.]*

Actus Quintus

Scaena 1. (Before the Temples of Mars, Venus, and Diana.)

[Enter Thesius, Perithous, Hipolita, attendants.]

THESEUS.

Now let'em enter, and before the gods
Tender their holy prayers: Let the Temples
Burne bright with sacred fires, and the Altars
In hallowed clouds commend their swelling Incense
To those above us: Let no due be wanting; *[Florish of Cornets.]*
They have a noble worke in hand, will honour
The very powers that love 'em.

[Enter Palamon and Arcite, and their Knights.]

PERITHOUS.

Sir, they enter.

THESEUS.

You valiant and strong harted Enemies,
You royall German foes, that this day come
To blow that furnesse out that flames betweene ye:
Lay by your anger for an houre, and dove–like,
Before the holy Altars of your helpers,
(The all feard gods) bow downe your stubborne bodies.
Your ire is more than mortall; So your helpe be,
And as the gods regard ye, fight with Iustice;

Ile leave you to your prayers, and betwixt ye
I part my wishes.

PERITHOUS.

Honour crowne the worthiest. *[Exit Theseus, and his traine.]*

PALAMON.

The glasse is running now that cannot finish
Till one of us expire: Thinke you but thus,
That were there ought in me which strove to show
Mine enemy in this businesse, wer't one eye
Against another, Arme opprest by Arme,
I would destroy th'offender, Coz, I would,
Though parcell of my selfe: Then from this gather
How I should tender you.

ARCITE.

I am in labour
To push your name, your auncient love, our kindred
Out of my memory; and i'th selfe same place
To seate something I would confound: So hoyst we
The sayles, that must these vessells port even where
The heavenly Lymiter pleases.

PALAMON.

You speake well;
Before I turne, Let me embrace thee, Cosen:
This I shall never doe agen.

ARCITE.

One farewell.

PALAMON.

Why, let it be so: Farewell, Coz. *[Exeunt Palamon and his Knights.]*

ARCITE.

Farewell, Sir.—
Knights, Kinsemen, Lovers, yea, my Sacrifices,
True worshippers of Mars, whose spirit in you
Expells the seedes of feare, and th'apprehension
Which still is farther off it, Goe with me
Before the god of our profession: There
Require of him the hearts of Lyons, and
The breath of Tigers, yea, the fearcenesse too,
Yea, the speed also,—to goe on, I meane,
Else wish we to be Snayles: you know my prize
Must be drag'd out of blood; force and great feate
Must put my Garland on, where she stickes
The Queene of Flowers: our intercession then
Must be to him that makes the Campe a Cestron
Brymd with the blood of men: give me your aide
And bend your spirits towards him. *[They kneele.]*
Thou mighty one, that with thy power hast turnd
Greene Neptune into purple, (whose Approach)
Comets prewarne, whose havocke in vaste Feild
Vnearthed skulls proclaime, whose breath blowes downe,
The teeming Ceres foyzon, who doth plucke
With hand armypotent from forth blew clowdes
The masond Turrets, that both mak'st and break'st
The stony girthes of Citties: me thy puple,
Yongest follower of thy Drom, instruct this day
With military skill, that to thy lawde
I may advance my Streamer, and by thee,
Be stil'd the Lord o'th day: give me, great Mars,

Some token of thy pleasure.

[Here they fall on their faces as formerly, and there is heard
clanging of Armor, with a short Thunder as the burst of a
Battaile,
whereupon they all rise and bow to the Altar.]

O Great Corrector of enormous times,
Shaker of ore–rank States, thou grand decider
Of dustie and old tytles, that healst with blood
The earth when it is sicke, and curst the world
O'th pluresie of people; I doe take
Thy signes auspiciously, and in thy name
To my designe march boldly. Let us goe. *[Exeunt.]*

[Enter Palamon and his Knights, with the former observance.]

PALAMON.

Our stars must glister with new fire, or be
To daie extinct; our argument is love,
Which if the goddesse of it grant, she gives
Victory too: then blend your spirits with mine,
You, whose free noblenesse doe make my cause
Your personall hazard; to the goddesse Venus
Commend we our proceeding, and implore
Her power unto our partie. *[Here they kneele as formerly.]*
Haile, Soveraigne Queene of secrets, who hast power
To call the feircest Tyrant from his rage,
And weepe unto a Girle; that ha'st the might,
Even with an ey–glance, to choke Marsis Drom
And turne th'allarme to whispers; that canst make
A Criple florish with his Crutch, and cure him
Before Apollo; that may'st force the King
To be his subjects vassaile, and induce
Stale gravitie to daunce; the pould Bachelour—

144

Whose youth, like wonton Boyes through Bonfyres,
Have skipt thy flame—at seaventy thou canst catch
And make him, to the scorne of his hoarse throate,
Abuse yong laies of love: what godlike power
Hast thou not power upon? To Phoebus thou
Add'st flames hotter then his; the heavenly fyres
Did scortch his mortall Son, thine him; the huntresse
All moyst and cold, some say, began to throw
Her Bow away, and sigh. Take to thy grace
Me, thy vowd Souldier, who doe beare thy yoke
As t'wer a wreath of Roses, yet is heavier
Then Lead it selfe, stings more than Nettles.
I have never beene foule mouthd against thy law,
Nev'r reveald secret, for I knew none—would not,
Had I kend all that were; I never practised
Vpon mans wife, nor would the Libells reade
Of liberall wits; I never at great feastes
Sought to betray a Beautie, but have blush'd
At simpring Sirs that did; I have beene harsh
To large Confessors, and have hotly ask'd them
If they had Mothers: I had one, a woman,
And women t'wer they wrong'd. I knew a man
Of eightie winters, this I told them, who
A Lasse of foureteene brided; twas thy power
To put life into dust; the aged Crampe
Had screw'd his square foote round,
The Gout had knit his fingers into knots,
Torturing Convulsions from his globie eyes,
Had almost drawne their spheeres, that what was life
In him seem'd torture: this Anatomie
Had by his yong faire pheare a Boy, and I
Beleev'd it was him, for she swore it was,
And who would not beleeve her? briefe, I am
To those that prate and have done no Companion;
To those that boast and have not a defyer;
To those that would and cannot a Rejoycer.

Yea, him I doe not love, that tells close offices
The fowlest way, nor names concealements in
The boldest language: such a one I am,
And vow that lover never yet made sigh
Truer then I. O, then, most soft, sweet goddesse,
Give me the victory of this question, which
Is true loves merit, and blesse me with a signe
Of thy great pleasure.

[Here Musicke is heard, Doves are seene to flutter; they fall againe upon their faces, then on their knees.]

PALAMON.

O thou, that from eleven to ninetie raign'st
In mortall bosomes, whose chase is this world,
And we in heards thy game: I give thee thankes
For this faire Token, which, being layd unto
Mine innocent true heart, armes in assurance *[They bow.]*
My body to this businesse. Let us rise
And bow before the goddesse: Time comes on. *[Exeunt.]*

[Still Musicke of Records.]

[Enter Emilia in white, her haire about her shoulders, (wearing) a wheaten wreath: One in white holding up her traine, her haire stucke with flowers: One before her carrying a silver Hynde, in which is conveyd Incense and sweet odours, which being set upon the Altar (of Diana) her maides standing a loofe, she sets fire to it; then they curtsey and kneele.]

EMILIA.

O sacred, shadowie, cold and constant Queene,
Abandoner of Revells, mute, contemplative,
Sweet, solitary, white as chaste, and pure

146

As windefand Snow, who to thy femall knights
Alow'st no more blood than will make a blush,
Which is their orders robe: I heere, thy Priest,
Am humbled fore thine Altar; O vouchsafe,
With that thy rare greene eye, which never yet
Beheld thing maculate, looke on thy virgin;
And, sacred silver Mistris, lend thine eare
(Which nev'r heard scurrill terme, into whose port
Ne're entred wanton found,) to my petition
Seasond with holy feare: This is my last
Of vestall office; I am bride habited,
But mayden harted, a husband I have pointed,
But doe not know him; out of two I should
Choose one and pray for his successe, but I
Am guiltlesse of election: of mine eyes,
Were I to loose one, they are equall precious,
I could doombe neither, that which perish'd should
Goe too't unsentenc'd: Therefore, most modest Queene,
He of the two Pretenders, that best loves me
And has the truest title in't, Let him
Take off my wheaten Gerland, or else grant
The fyle and qualitie I hold, I may
Continue in thy Band.

*[Here the Hynde vanishes under the Altar: and in the place ascends
a Rose Tree, having one Rose upon it.]*

See what our Generall of Ebbs and Flowes
Out from the bowells of her holy Altar
With sacred act advances! But one Rose:
If well inspird, this Battaile shal confound
Both these brave Knights, and I, a virgin flowre
Must grow alone unpluck'd.

*[Here is heard a sodaine twang of Instruments, and the Rose fals\
from the Tree (which vanishes under the altar.)]*

The flowre is falne, the Tree descends: O, Mistris,
Thou here dischargest me; I shall be gather'd:
I thinke so, but I know not thine owne will;
Vnclaspe thy Misterie.—I hope she's pleas'd,
Her Signes were gratious. *[They curtsey and Exeunt.]*

Scaena 2. (A darkened Room in the Prison.)

[Enter Doctor, Iaylor and Wooer, in habite of Palamon.]

DOCTOR.

Has this advice I told you, done any good upon her?

WOOER.

O very much; The maids that kept her company
Have halfe perswaded her that I am Palamon;
Within this halfe houre she came smiling to me,
And asked me what I would eate, and when I would kisse her:
I told her presently, and kist her twice.

DOCTOR.

Twas well done; twentie times had bin far better,
For there the cure lies mainely.

WOOER.

Then she told me
She would watch with me to night, for well she knew
What houre my fit would take me.

DOCTOR.

Let her doe so,
And when your fit comes, fit her home,
And presently.

WOOER.

She would have me sing.

DOCTOR.

You did so?

WOOER.

No.

DOCTOR.

Twas very ill done, then;
You should observe her ev'ry way.

WOOER.

Alas,
I have no voice, Sir, to confirme her that way.

DOCTOR.

That's all one, if yee make a noyse;

If she intreate againe, doe any thing,—
Lye with her, if she aske you.

IAILOR.

Hoa, there, Doctor!

DOCTOR.

Yes, in the waie of cure.

IAILOR.

But first, by your leave,
I'th way of honestie.

DOCTOR.

That's but a nicenesse,
Nev'r cast your child away for honestie;
Cure her first this way, then if shee will be honest,
She has the path before her.

IAILOR.

Thanke yee, Doctor.

DOCTOR.

Pray, bring her in,
And let's see how shee is.

IAILOR.

I will, and tell her
Her Palamon staies for her: But, Doctor,

Me thinkes you are i'th wrong still. *[Exit Iaylor.]*

DOCTOR.

Goe, goe:
You Fathers are fine Fooles: her honesty?
And we should give her physicke till we finde that—

WOOER.

Why, doe you thinke she is not honest, Sir?

DOCTOR.

How old is she?

WOOER.

She's eighteene.

DOCTOR.

She may be,
But that's all one; tis nothing to our purpose.
What ere her Father saies, if you perceave
Her moode inclining that way that I spoke of,
Videlicet, the way of flesh—you have me?

WOOER.

Yet, very well, Sir.

DOCTOR.

Please her appetite,
And doe it home; it cures her, ipso facto,

The mellencholly humour that infects her.

WOOER.

I am of your minde, Doctor.

[Enter Iaylor, Daughter, Maide.]

DOCTOR.

You'l finde it so; she comes, pray humour her.

IAILOR.

Come, your Love Palamon staies for you, childe,
And has done this long houre, to visite you.

DAUGHTER.

I thanke him for his gentle patience;
He's a kind Gentleman, and I am much bound to him.
Did you nev'r see the horse he gave me?

IAILOR.

Yes.

DAUGHTER.

How doe you like him?

IAILOR.

He's a very faire one.

DAUGHTER.

You never saw him dance?

IAILOR.

No.

DAUGHTER.

I have often.
He daunces very finely, very comely,
And for a Iigge, come cut and long taile to him,
He turnes ye like a Top.

IAILOR.

That's fine, indeede.

DAUGHTER.

Hee'l dance the Morris twenty mile an houre,
And that will founder the best hobby–horse
(If I have any skill) in all the parish,
And gallops to the turne of LIGHT A' LOVE:
What thinke you of this horse?

IAILOR.

Having these vertues,
I thinke he might be broght to play at Tennis.

DAUGHTER.

Alas, that's nothing.

IAILOR.

Can he write and reade too?

DAUGHTER.

A very faire hand, and casts himselfe th'accounts
Of all his hay and provender: That Hostler
Must rise betime that cozens him. You know
The Chestnut Mare the Duke has?

IAILOR.

Very well.

DAUGHTER.

She is horribly in love with him, poore beast,
But he is like his master, coy and scornefull.

IAILOR.

What dowry has she?

DAUGHTER.

Some two hundred Bottles,
And twenty strike of Oates; but hee'l ne're have her;
He lispes in's neighing, able to entice
A Millars Mare: Hee'l be the death of her.

DOCTOR.

What stuffe she utters!

IAILOR.

Make curtsie; here your love comes.

WOOER.

Pretty soule,
How doe ye? that's a fine maide, ther's a curtsie!

DAUGHTER.

Yours to command ith way of honestie.
How far is't now to'th end o'th world, my Masters?

DOCTOR.

Why, a daies Iorney, wench.

DAUGHTER.

Will you goe with me?

WOOER.

What shall we doe there, wench?

DAUGHTER.

Why, play at stoole ball:
What is there else to doe?

WOOER.

I am content,
If we shall keepe our wedding there.

DAUGHTER.

Tis true:
For there, I will assure you, we shall finde
Some blind Priest for the purpose, that will venture
To marry us, for here they are nice, and foolish;
Besides, my father must be hang'd to morrow
And that would be a blot i'th businesse.
Are not you Palamon?

WOOER.

Doe not you know me?

DAUGHTER.

Yes, but you care not for me; I have nothing
But this pore petticoate, and too corse Smockes.

WOOER.

That's all one; I will have you.

DAUGHTER.

Will you surely?

WOOER.

Yes, by this faire hand, will I.

DAUGHTER.

Wee'l to bed, then.

WOOER.

Ev'n when you will. *[Kisses her.]*

DAUGHTER.

O Sir, you would faine be nibling.

WOOER.

Why doe you rub my kisse off?

DAUGHTER.

Tis a sweet one,
And will perfume me finely against the wedding.
Is not this your Cosen Arcite?

DOCTOR.

Yes, sweet heart,
And I am glad my Cosen Palamon
Has made so faire a choice.

DAUGHTER.

Doe you thinke hee'l have me?

DOCTOR.

Yes, without doubt.

DAUGHTER.

Doe you thinke so too?

IAILOR.

Yes.

DAUGHTER.

We shall have many children:—Lord, how y'ar growne!
My Palamon, I hope, will grow, too, finely,
Now he's at liberty: Alas, poore Chicken,
He was kept downe with hard meate and ill lodging,
But ile kisse him up againe.

[Emter a Messenger.]

MESSENGER.

What doe you here? you'l loose the noblest sight
That ev'r was seene.

IAILOR.

Are they i'th Field?

MESSENGER.

They are.
You beare a charge there too.

IAILOR.

Ile away straight.
I must ev'n leave you here.

DOCTOR.

Nay, wee'l goe with you;
I will not loose the Fight.

IAILOR.

How did you like her?

DOCTOR.

Ile warrant you, within these 3. or 4. daies
Ile make her right againe. You must not from her,
But still preserve her in this way.

WOOER.

I will.

DOCTOR.

Lets get her in.

WOOER.

Come, sweete, wee'l goe to dinner;
And then weele play at Cardes.

DAUGHTER.

And shall we kisse too?

WOOER.

A hundred times.

DAUGHTER.

And twenty.

WOOER.

I, and twenty.

DAUGHTER.

And then wee'l sleepe together.

DOCTOR.

Take her offer.

WOOER.

Yes, marry, will we.

DAUGHTER.

But you shall not hurt me.

WOOER.

I will not, sweete.

DAUGHTER.

If you doe, Love, ile cry. *[Florish. Exeunt]*

Scaena 3. (A Place near the Lists.)

[Enter Theseus, Hipolita, Emilia, Perithous: and some Attendants,

(T. Tucke: Curtis.)]

EMILIA.

Ile no step further.

PERITHOUS.

Will you loose this sight?

EMILIA.

I had rather see a wren hawke at a fly
Then this decision; ev'ry blow that falls
Threats a brave life, each stroake laments
The place whereon it fals, and sounds more like
A Bell then blade: I will stay here;
It is enough my hearing shall be punishd
With what shall happen—gainst the which there is
No deaffing, but to heare—not taint mine eye
With dread sights, it may shun.

PERITHOUS.

Sir, my good Lord,
Your Sister will no further.

THESEUS.

Oh, she must.
She shall see deeds of honour in their kinde,
Which sometime show well, pencild. Nature now
Shall make and act the Story, the beleife
Both seald with eye and eare; you must be present,
You are the victours meede, the price, and garlond
To crowne the Questions title.

EMILIA.

Pardon me;
If I were there, I'ld winke.

THESEUS.

You must be there;
This Tryall is as t'wer i'th night, and you
The onely star to shine.

EMILIA.

I am extinct;
There is but envy in that light, which showes
The one the other: darkenes, which ever was
The dam of horrour, who do's stand accurst
Of many mortall Millions, may even now,
By casting her blacke mantle over both,
That neither coulde finde other, get her selfe
Some part of a good name, and many a murther
Set off wherto she's guilty.

HIPPOLITA.

You must goe.

EMILIA.

In faith, I will not.

THESEUS.

Why, the knights must kindle
Their valour at your eye: know, of this war

You are the Treasure, and must needes be by
To give the Service pay.

EMILIA.

Sir, pardon me;
The tytle of a kingdome may be tride
Out of it selfe.

THESEUS.

Well, well, then, at your pleasure;
Those that remaine with you could wish their office
To any of their Enemies.

HIPPOLITA.

Farewell, Sister;
I am like to know your husband fore your selfe
By some small start of time: he whom the gods
Doe of the two know best, I pray them he
Be made your Lot.

[Exeunt Theseus, Hipolita, Perithous, c.]

EMILIA.

Arcite is gently visagd; yet his eye
Is like an Engyn bent, or a sharpe weapon
In a soft sheath; mercy and manly courage
Are bedfellowes in his visage. Palamon
Has a most menacing aspect: his brow
Is grav'd, and seemes to bury what it frownes on;
Yet sometime tis not so, but alters to
The quallity of his thoughts; long time his eye
Will dwell upon his object. Mellencholly

Becomes him nobly; So do's Arcites mirth,
But Palamons sadnes is a kinde of mirth,
So mingled, as if mirth did make him sad,
And sadnes, merry; those darker humours that
Sticke misbecomingly on others, on them
Live in faire dwelling. *[Cornets. Trompets sound as to a charge.]*
Harke, how yon spurs to spirit doe incite
The Princes to their proofe! Arcite may win me,
And yet may Palamon wound Arcite to
The spoyling of his figure. O, what pitty
Enough for such a chance; if I were by,
I might doe hurt, for they would glance their eies
Toward my Seat, and in that motion might
Omit a ward, or forfeit an offence
Which crav'd that very time: it is much better
I am not there; oh better never borne
Then minister to such harme. *[Cornets. A great cry and noice within, crying 'a Palamon'.]* What is the chance?

[Enter Servant.]

SERVANT.

The Crie's 'a Palamon'.

EMILIA.

Then he has won! Twas ever likely;
He lookd all grace and successe, and he is
Doubtlesse the prim'st of men: I pre'thee, run
And tell me how it goes. *[Showt, and Cornets: Crying, 'a Palamon.']*

SERVANT.

Still Palamon.

EMILIA.

Run and enquire. Poore Servant, thou hast lost;
Vpon my right side still I wore thy picture,
Palamons on the left: why so, I know not;
I had no end in't else, chance would have it so.
On the sinister side the heart lyes; Palamon
Had the best boding chance. *[Another cry, and showt within, and Cornets.]* This burst of clamour
Is sure th'end o'th Combat.

[Enter Servant.]

SERVANT.

They saide that Palamon had Arcites body
Within an inch o'th Pyramid, that the cry
Was generall 'a Palamon': But, anon,
Th'Assistants made a brave redemption, and
The two bold Tytlers, at this instant are
Hand to hand at it.

EMILIA.

Were they metamorphisd
Both into one! oh why? there were no woman
Worth so composd a Man: their single share,
Their noblenes peculier to them, gives
The prejudice of disparity, values shortnes, *[Cornets. Cry within, Arcite, Arcite.]*
To any Lady breathing—More exulting?
Palamon still?

SERVANT.

Nay, now the sound is Arcite.

EMILIA.

I pre'thee, lay attention to the Cry, *[Cornets. A great showt and cry, 'Arcite, victory!']*
Set both thine eares to'th busines.

SERVANT.

The cry is
'Arcite', and 'victory', harke: 'Arcite, victory!'
The Combats consummation is proclaim'd
By the wind Instruments.

EMILIA.

Halfe sights saw
That Arcite was no babe; god's lyd, his richnes
And costlines of spirit look't through him, it could
No more be hid in him then fire in flax,
Then humble banckes can goe to law with waters,
That drift windes force to raging: I did thinke
Good Palamon would miscarry; yet I knew not
Why I did thinke so; Our reasons are not prophets,
When oft our fancies are. They are comming off:
Alas, poore Palamon! *[Cornets.]*

[Enter Theseus, Hipolita, Pirithous, Arcite as victor, and attendants, c.]

THESEUS.

Lo, where our Sister is in expectation,
Yet quaking, and unsetled.—Fairest Emily,

166

The gods by their divine arbitrament
Have given you this Knight; he is a good one
As ever strooke at head. Give me your hands;
Receive you her, you him; be plighted with
A love that growes, as you decay.

ARCITE.

Emily,
To buy you, I have lost what's deerest to me,
Save what is bought, and yet I purchase cheapely,
As I doe rate your value.

THESEUS.

O loved Sister,
He speakes now of as brave a Knight as ere
Did spur a noble Steed: Surely, the gods
Would have him die a Batchelour, least his race
Should shew i'th world too godlike: His behaviour
So charmed me, that me thought Alcides was
To him a sow of lead: if I could praise
Each part of him to'th all I have spoke, your Arcite
Did not loose by't; For he that was thus good
Encountred yet his Better. I have heard
Two emulous Philomels beate the eare o'th night
With their contentious throates, now one the higher,
Anon the other, then againe the first,
And by and by out breasted, that the sence
Could not be judge betweene 'em: So it far'd
Good space betweene these kinesmen; till heavens did
Make hardly one the winner. Weare the Girlond
With joy that you have won: For the subdude,
Give them our present Iustice, since I know
Their lives but pinch 'em; Let it here be done.
The Sceane's not for our seeing, goe we hence,

Right joyfull, with some sorrow.—Arme your prize,
I know you will not loose her.—Hipolita,
I see one eye of yours conceives a teare
The which it will deliver. *[Florish.]*

EMILIA.

Is this wynning?
Oh all you heavenly powers, where is your mercy?
But that your wils have saide it must be so,
And charge me live to comfort this unfriended,
This miserable Prince, that cuts away
A life more worthy from him then all women,
I should, and would, die too.

HIPPOLITA.

Infinite pitty,
That fowre such eies should be so fixd on one
That two must needes be blinde fort.

THESEUS.

So it is. *[Exeunt.]*

Scaena 4. (The same; a Block prepared.)

[Enter Palamon and his Knightes pyniond: Iaylor, Executioner, c. Gard.]

(PALAMON.)

Ther's many a man alive that hath out liv'd
The love o'th people; yea, i'th selfesame state
Stands many a Father with his childe; some comfort
We have by so considering: we expire
And not without mens pitty. To live still,
Have their good wishes; we prevent
The loathsome misery of age, beguile
The Gowt and Rheume, that in lag howres attend
For grey approachers; we come towards the gods
Yong and unwapper'd, not halting under Crymes
Many and stale: that sure shall please the gods,
Sooner than such, to give us Nectar with 'em,
For we are more cleare Spirits. My deare kinesmen,
Whose lives (for this poore comfort) are laid downe,
You have sould 'em too too cheape.

1. KNIGHT.

What ending could be
Of more content? ore us the victors have
Fortune, whose title is as momentary,
As to us death is certaine: A graine of honour
They not ore'–weigh us.

2. KNIGHT.

Let us bid farewell;
And with our patience anger tottring Fortune,
Who at her certain'st reeles.

3. KNIGHT.

Come; who begins?

PALAMON.

Ev'n he that led you to this Banket shall
Taste to you all.—Ah ha, my Friend, my Friend,
Your gentle daughter gave me freedome once;
You'l see't done now for ever: pray, how do'es she?
I heard she was not well; her kind of ill
Gave me some sorrow.

IAILOR.

Sir, she's well restor'd,
And to be marryed shortly.

PALAMON.

By my short life,
I am most glad on't; Tis the latest thing
I shall be glad of; pre'thee tell her so:
Commend me to her, and to peece her portion,
Tender her this. *[Gives purse.]*

1. KNIGHT.

Nay lets be offerers all.

2. KNIGHT.

Is it a maide?

PALAMON.

Verily, I thinke so,
A right good creature, more to me deserving
Then I can quight or speake of.

ALL KNIGHTS.

Commend us to her. *[They give their purses.]*

IAILOR.

The gods requight you all,
And make her thankefull.

PALAMON.

Adiew; and let my life be now as short,
As my leave taking. *[Lies on the Blocke.]*

1. KNIGHT.

Leade, couragious Cosin.

2. KNIGHT.

Wee'l follow cheerefully. *[A great noise within crying, 'run, save, hold!']*

[Enter in hast a Messenger.]

MESSENGER.

Hold, hold! O hold, hold, hold!

[Enter Pirithous in haste.]

PERITHOUS.

Hold! hoa! It is a cursed hast you made,
If you have done so quickly. Noble Palamon,

The gods will shew their glory in a life,
That thou art yet to leade.

PALAMON.

Can that be,
When Venus, I have said, is false? How doe things fare?

PERITHOUS.

Arise, great Sir, and give the tydings eare
That are most dearly sweet and bitter.

PALAMON.

What
Hath wakt us from our dreame?

PERITHOUS.

List then: your Cosen,
Mounted upon a Steed that Emily
Did first bestow on him, a blacke one, owing
Not a hayre worth of white—which some will say
Weakens his price, and many will not buy
His goodnesse with this note: Which superstition
Heere findes allowance—On this horse is Arcite
Trotting the stones of Athens, which the Calkins
Did rather tell then trample; for the horse
Would make his length a mile, if't pleas'd his Rider
To put pride in him: as he thus went counting
The flinty pavement, dancing, as t'wer, to'th Musicke
His owne hoofes made; (for as they say from iron
Came Musickes origen) what envious Flint,
Cold as old Saturne, and like him possest
With fire malevolent, darted a Sparke,

Or what feirce sulphur else, to this end made,
I comment not;—the hot horse, hot as fire,
Tooke Toy at this, and fell to what disorder
His power could give his will; bounds, comes on end,
Forgets schoole dooing, being therein traind,
And of kind mannadge; pig–like he whines
At the sharpe Rowell, which he freats at rather
Then any jot obaies; seekes all foule meanes
Of boystrous and rough Iadrie, to dis–seate
His Lord, that kept it bravely: when nought serv'd,
When neither Curb would cracke, girth breake nor diffring plunges
Dis–roote his Rider whence he grew, but that
He kept him tweene his legges, on his hind hoofes on end he stands,
That Arcites leggs, being higher then his head,
Seem'd with strange art to hand: His victors wreath
Even then fell off his head: and presently
Backeward the Iade comes ore, and his full poyze
Becomes the Riders loade: yet is he living,
But such a vessell tis, that floates but for
The surge that next approaches: he much desires
To have some speech with you: Loe he appeares.

[Enter Theseus, Hipolita, Emilia, Arcite in a chaire.]

PALAMON.

O miserable end of our alliance!
The gods are mightie, Arcite: if thy heart,
Thy worthie, manly heart, be yet unbroken,
Give me thy last words; I am Palamon,
One that yet loves thee dying.

ARCITE.

Take Emilia
And with her all the worlds joy: Reach thy hand:

Farewell: I have told my last houre. I was false,
Yet never treacherous: Forgive me, Cosen:—
One kisse from faire Emilia: Tis done:
Take her: I die.

PALAMON.

Thy brave soule seeke Elizium.

EMILIA.

Ile close thine eyes, Prince; blessed soules be with thee!
Thou art a right good man, and while I live,
This day I give to teares.

PALAMON.

And I to honour.

THESEUS.

In this place first you fought: ev'n very here
I sundred you: acknowledge to the gods
Our thankes that you are living.
His part is playd, and though it were too short,
He did it well: your day is lengthned, and
The blissefull dew of heaven do's arowze you.
The powerfull Venus well hath grac'd her Altar,
And given you your love: Our Master Mars
Hath vouch'd his Oracle, and to Arcite gave
The grace of the Contention: So the Deities
Have shewd due justice: Beare this hence.

PALAMON.

O Cosen,

That we should things desire, which doe cost us
The losse of our desire! That nought could buy
Deare love, but losse of deare love!

THESEUS.

Never Fortune
Did play a subtler Game: The conquerd triumphes,
The victor has the Losse: yet in the passage
The gods have beene most equall: Palamon,
Your kinseman hath confest the right o'th Lady
Did lye in you, for you first saw her, and
Even then proclaimd your fancie: He restord her
As your stolne Iewell, and desir'd your spirit
To send him hence forgiven; The gods my justice
Take from my hand, and they themselves become
The Executioners: Leade your Lady off;
And call your Lovers from the stage of death,
Whom I adopt my Frinds. A day or two
Let us looke sadly, and give grace unto
The Funerall of Arcite; in whose end
The visages of Bridegroomes weele put on
And smile with Palamon; for whom an houre,
But one houre, since, I was as dearely sorry,
As glad of Arcite: and am now as glad,
As for him sorry. O you heavenly Charmers,
What things you make of us! For what we lacke
We laugh, for what we have, are sorry: still
Are children in some kind. Let us be thankefull
For that which is, and with you leave dispute
That are above our question. Let's goe off,
And beare us like the time. *[Florish. Exeunt.]*

EPILOGVE

I would now aske ye how ye like the Play,
But, as it is with Schoole Boyes, cannot say,
I am cruell fearefull: pray, yet stay a while,
And let me looke upon ye: No man smile?
Then it goes hard, I see; He that has
Lov'd a yong hansome wench, then, show his face—
Tis strange if none be heere—and if he will
Against his Conscience, let him hisse, and kill
Our Market: Tis in vaine, I see, to stay yee;
Have at the worst can come, then! Now what say ye?
And yet mistake me not: I am not bold;
We have no such cause. If the tale we have told
(For tis no other) any way content ye
(For to that honest purpose it was ment ye)
We have our end; and ye shall have ere long,
I dare say, many a better, to prolong
Your old loves to us: we, and all our might
Rest at your service. Gentlemen, good night. *[Florish.]*

FINIS

Printed in the United States
79107LV00004B/49